MW01703533

Microsoft® Windows® XP Guide

Addendum to Enhanced A+ Guide to Managing and Maintaining Your PC

Enhanced Third Edition

Jean Andrews

COURSE TECHNOLOGY
THOMSON LEARNING™

Australia • Canada • Mexico • Singapore • Spain • United Kingdom • United States

COURSE TECHNOLOGY
THOMSON LEARNING™

Microsoft® Windows® XP Guide: Addendum to Enhanced A+ Guide to Managing and Maintaining Your PC, Enhanced Third Edition

by Jean Andrews

Senior Editor
Lisa Egan

Managing Editor
Jennifer Locke

Production Group Leader
Jennifer Goguen

Developmental Editor
Deb Kaufmann

Editorial Assistant
Nick Lombardi

Marketing Manager
Jason Sakos

Associate Manufacturing Manager
Denise Sandler

Senior Inventory Systems Coordinator
Eric Masters

Inventory Manager
Ted Gibbons

Compositor
GEX Publishing Services

Cover Designer
Janet Lavine

COPYRIGHT © 2002 Course Technology, a division of Thomson Learning
Thomson Learning™ is a trademark used herein under license.

Printed in Canada

2 3 4 5 6 7 8 9 WC 06 05 04 03 02

For more information, contact Course Technology, 25 Thomson Place, Boston, Massachusetts, 02210.
Or find us on the World Wide Web at: www.course.com

ALL RIGHTS RESERVED. No part of this work may be reproduced, transcribed, or used in any form or by any means—graphic, electronic, or mechanical, including photocopying, recording, taping, Web distribution, or information storage and retrieval systems—without prior written permission of the publisher.

For permission to use material from this text or product, contact us by
Tel (800) 730-2214
Fax (800) 730-2215
www.thomsonrights.com

Disclaimer
Course Technology reserves the right to revise this publication and make changes from time to time in its content without notice.

A+ is a registered trademark of CompTIA.

ISBN 0-619-13063-6

TABLE OF

Contents

Introduction

Microsoft® Windows® XP Guide

Addendum to Enhanced A+ Guide to Managing and Maintaining Your PC

The *Microsoft Windows XP Guide* contains a new chapter and lab exercises on Windows XP, and is meant to accompany *Enhanced A+ Guide to Managing and Maintaining Your PC*. The Windows XP guide is the next chapter—Chapter 21—of *Enhanced A+ Guide to Managing and Maintaining Your PC*. It builds upon the material in this core book and provides an in-depth look at installing, supporting, and troubleshooting Windows XP Professional. Plenty of screenshots and step-by-step instructions guide students through the installation and maintenance of Windows XP. In addition, there are five new hands-on labs using Windows XP. This updated coverage is written by best-selling author and instructor Jean Andrews.

For more information about *Enhanced A+ Guide to Managing and Maintaining Your PC*, please contact your sales representative or go to www.course.com/pcrepair.

CHAPTER

21

SUPPORTING WINDOWS XP PROFESSIONAL

In this chapter, you will learn:

- About the basic features, advantages, and disadvantages of Windows XP
- About the architecture of Windows XP
- How to install Windows XP
- How to use Windows XP
- How to install hardware and applications with Windows XP
- How to troubleshoot the Windows XP boot process
- About tools for troubleshooting and maintaining Windows XP

Windows XP is the latest generation of Microsoft operating systems. Windows XP currently comes as Windows XP Home Edition, Windows XP Professional, and Windows XP 64-bit Edition. Windows XP is expected to first replace Windows 9x and then replace Windows 2000. This guide focuses on Windows XP Professional, which is considered the next upgrade of Windows 2000 Professional, and builds the foundation you will need to understand and support the OS.

Features of Windows XP

Windows XP attempts to accomplish integration of 9x and 2000 while providing added support for digital and networking technologies. Windows XP Home and Windows XP Professional share these features, among others:

- A new user interface that has a different look from the desktops for earlier Windows versions such as Windows 9x and Windows NT
- The ability for two users to be logged on simultaneously, both with their own applications open
- Windows Media Player for Windows XP, which provides a centralized application for working with digital media
- Windows Messenger for instant messaging, conferencing, and application sharing
- An expanded help feature
- Advanced security features

Here are some of the features that Windows XP Professional adds to the Home Edition:

- Features for remote access, including remote desktop and roaming user profiles
- Additional security features
- Multilingual capabilities
- Support for new higher performance processors

There is also Windows XP 64-bit Edition designed to be used with a high-end CPU such as the Intel Itanium. This version of Windows XP is designed mostly for servers or heavily technical workstation users who need greater amounts of memory and higher performance than standard desktop users, for example, for scientific and engineering applications. For instance, an aircraft designer who needs to simulate how various conditions affect aircraft materials might use Windows XP on a system supporting resource-intensive simulation and animation applications.

Windows Internet Explorer, Windows Media Player, a firewall, and other Microsoft products are tightly integrated with the XP operating system. Some users see this as a disadvantage and others see it as an advantage. Full evaluation of the integration of Microsoft software with the Windows XP operating system is beyond the scope of this overview.

> TIP: Remember that the requirements of an OS will vary depending on which version you have installed and what applications and hardware you have installed with it.

Windows XP provides several enhancements over Windows 2000 and other earlier versions. Table 1-8 summarizes the advantages and disadvantages of Windows XP.

Table 21-1 Advantages and disadvantages of Windows XP

Advantages	Disadvantages
• Provides better integration of Windows 9x and NT than did Windows 2000. • Offers significant GUI enhancements over earlier versions of Windows. • Adds features but uses only slightly more total memory for the OS than does Windows 2000. • Adds advanced file sorting options, such as sorting pictures by resolution or sound files by artist. • Includes built-in support for compressed files. • Has improved troubleshooting tools and is generally more stable than previous Windows OSs.	• Requires nearly a gigabyte of hard drive space for the operating system itself, and at least a 233 MHz processor with 64 MB of RAM. • Programs used with Windows XP may require more than the minimum system specifications for the operating system. • Nearly eliminates support for device drivers not approved by Microsoft. • Security concerns with centralized storage of online information in Microsoft Passport, a repository of the user IDs and passwords you use on the Internet.

THE WINDOWS XP ARCHITECTURE

Windows XP is an evolution of Windows NT and Windows 2000 and uses the same basic architecture. The look and feel of Windows XP is slightly different, and utilities and functions are organized differently under menus and windows. You'll see many of these differences later in this chapter.

Windows XP uses the same kernel architecture as Windows NT and Windows 2000. Figure 21-1 shows how the different OS components relate. Notice in the figure that some low-level device drivers such as those that access the hard drive have direct access to hardware, just as they do with Windows NT and Windows 2000. All 16-bit and 32-bit applications relate to the kernel by way of the Win32 subsystem operating in user mode. As you will see later in the chapter, the boot process is also the same, and the files needed for a successful boot are the same as those for Windows NT/2000.

Windows XP is generally more stable than Windows NT and Windows 2000. It was designed with the intention of avoiding situations with Windows NT/2000 that caused drivers and applications to bring these systems down. Installing Windows XP should also be an easier experience than installing either Windows NT or Windows 2000. In addition, Windows XP has increased security, including a built-in Internet firewall called Internet Connection Firewall that is designed to protect a home PC connected directly to the Internet by way of an always-on connection such as cable modem or DSL.

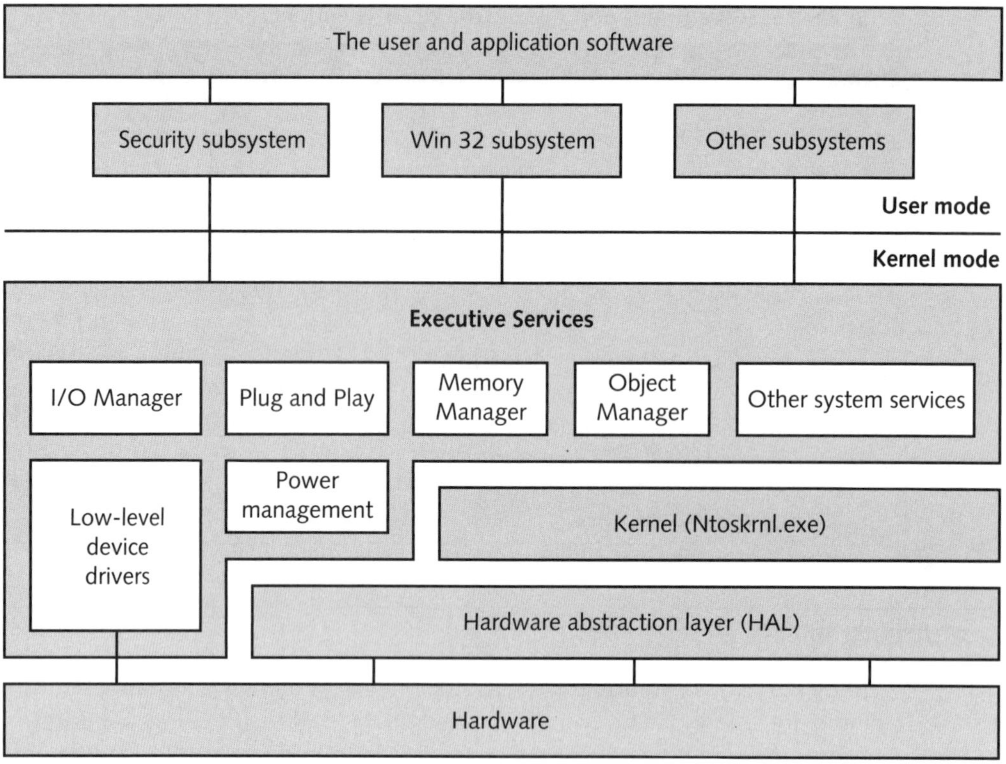

Figure 21-1 The Windows XP architecture uses the same basic structure and components as Windows NT and Windows 2000

INSTALLING WINDOWS XP

Installing Windows XP involves many of the same considerations and decisions that you learned about when installing Windows 2000. In this section, you will learn how to install Windows XP as a clean install and as an upgrade, including how to set up a dual boot.

Planning the Installation

Before installing Windows XP, do the following:

- Verify that the system meets the minimum and recommended requirements, shown in Table 21-2.
- Check the hardware compatibility list (HCL) to verify that all installed hardware components are compatible with Windows XP.
- Decide how you will partition your hard drive and what file system you will use.

- For a PC on a network, decide whether the PC will be configured as a workstation in a workgroup or as part of a domain.
- Make a final checklist to verify that you have done all the above and are ready to begin the installation.

Table 21-2 Minimum and recommended requirements for Windows XP Professional

Component or Device	Minimum Requirement	Recommended Requirement
One or two CPUs	Pentium II 233 MHz or better	Pentium II 300 MHz or better
RAM	64 MB	128 MB up to 4 GB
Hard drive partition	2 GB	2 GB or more
Free space on the hard drive partition	1.5 GB	2 GB or more
CD-ROM drive	12x	12x or faster
Accessories	Keyboard and mouse or other pointing device	Keyboard and mouse or other pointing device

Minimum Requirements and Hardware Compatibility

You can use the My Computer icon on the Windows desktop to determine the current CPU and available RAM. To see how much hard drive space is available, using Windows Explorer, right-click on the drive letter and select Properties from the shortcut menu. Part of the installation process for an upgrade is to clean up the hard drive, which might free up some hard drive space. Even though Windows XP requires only 640 MB to install, you will not be able to achieve acceptable results unless you have at least 1.5 GB of free hard drive space on the volume that holds Windows XP.

There are several ways you can verify that software and hardware qualify for Windows XP. One way is to run the Readiness Analyzer. Use this command from the Windows XP CD, substituting the drive letter for your CD-ROM drive for D in the command line:

```
D:\I386\Winnt32 /checkupgradeonly
```

Depending on the release of Windows XP, your path might be different. The process takes about 10 minutes to run and displays a report that can be saved and later printed. The default name and path of the report is C:\Windows\compat.txt. The report is important if you have software you are not sure will work under Windows XP. If the analyzer reports that your software will not work under Windows XP, you might choose to upgrade the software or set up a dual boot with your old OS and Windows XP (dual-boot setup is covered later in the chapter).

Readiness Analyzer also checks hardware compatibility. Another way to verify your hardware is to go to the Microsoft Web site at *www.microsoft.com/hcl*. Search on each hardware device by type (see Figure 21-2). There might be a copy of the Windows XP Professional HCL in the hcl.txt file on the Windows XP CD in the support folder. But for the most up-to-date information, use the Microsoft Web site.

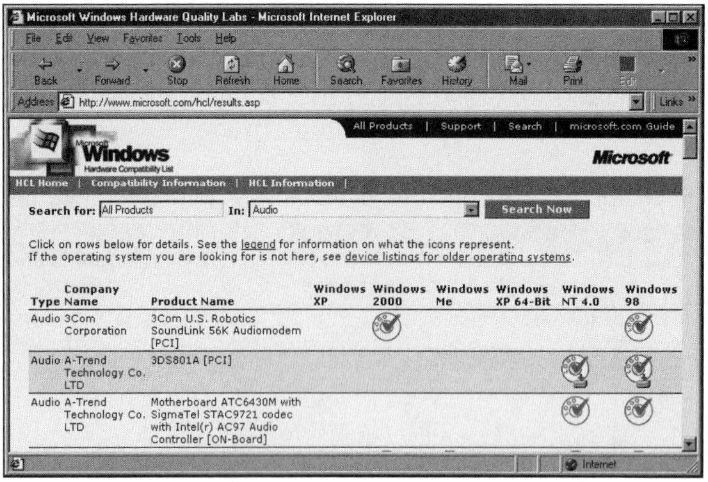

Figure 21-2 Search for each hardware component by type to determine if it qualifies for Windows XP

If your hardware does not qualify for Windows XP, check the hardware manufacturer's Web site for an upgrade and download the upgrade drivers before you begin the installation. If you plan to erase the hard drive as part of the installation, store these drivers on floppy disk or on a network drive until you're ready to install them under Windows XP. If you can't find an upgrade, sometimes a device will work if you substitute a Windows driver written for a similar device. Check the documentation for your device, looking for information about other devices it will emulate. It is especially important to know that your network card or modem card qualifies for Windows XP before you install the OS because you will need the card to access the Internet to get upgrades. If you are not sure an important hardware component qualifies, then install Windows XP as a dual boot with your current OS. Later, when you get the component working under Windows XP, you can uninstall the other OS.

Hard Drive Partitions and File Systems

Windows XP needs at least a 2-GB partition for the installation and should have about 1.5 GB of free space on that partition. You can install Windows XP on the same partition as another OS, but Windows XP will overwrite the existing OS on that partition. If you do not have a free 2-GB partition for the installation, you must delete smaller partitions and repartition the drive. Deleting a partition erases all data on that partition, so be sure to create backups first. Follow these general directions to ensure that partitions on the hard drive are adequate to install Windows XP:

- For Windows 9x, use Fdisk at the command prompt, and, for Windows 2000, use Disk Management to determine what partitions are on the drive, how large they are, what logical drives are assigned to them, and how much free space is on the drive that is not yet partitioned.

- If existing partitions are too small, look at the free space on the drive. If there is enough free space that is not yet partitioned, use that free space to create a new partition that is at least 2 GB.
- If you cannot create a 2-GB or larger partition, back up your data, delete the smaller partitions, and create a 2-GB active partition on the drive.
- If you have free space on the drive for other partitions, don't partition them at this time. First, install Windows XP and then use Disk Management under Windows XP to partition the remaining free space on the drive.

The same concerns about selecting a file system for Windows 2000 apply to Windows XP. The file systems supported by Windows XP are the same as those supported by Windows 2000: FAT16, FAT32, and NTFS. Recall that the NTFS file system used by Windows 2000 was incompatible with the Windows NT NTFS file system, making for a potential problem when installing Windows 2000 and Windows NT on the same PC as a dual boot. Because the Windows XP NTFS file system is the same as that of the Windows 2000 NTFS file system, a dual boot between these two OSs should not be a problem. Here are the general directions for selecting a file system:

- Use the NTFS file system if you are interested in file and folder security, file compression, control over how much disk space a user is allowed, or file encryption.
- Use the FAT16 or FAT32 file system if you are setting up a dual boot with Windows XP and Windows 9x, and each OS must access all partitions.
- Use the FAT16 file system if you are setting up a dual boot with MS-DOS or Windows NT and each OS must access all partitions.

Joining a Workgroup or a Domain

If you are installing Windows XP on a network, you must make decisions about how you will access the network. If you have less than 10 computers networked together, Microsoft recommends that you join these computers in a workgroup where each computer controls its own resources. In this case, each user account is set up on the local computer, independently from user accounts on other PCs. There is no centralized control of resources. For more than 10 computers, Microsoft recommends that you use a domain controller running a network operating system such as Windows 2000 Server to control resources on the network. (Windows XP Professional installed on a workstation can then be a client on this Windows network. Also, it is expected that Microsoft will soon release Windows XP Server.) You will also want to use a domain controller if you want to administer and secure the network from a centralized location or if there are several centralized resources on the network that are shared by many users.

Upgrade or Clean Install

If you plan to set up a dual boot, then you will perform a clean install for Windows XP. If you already have an OS installed and you do not plan a dual boot, then you have a choice between an upgrade and a clean install. Things to consider when making this decision are:

- You can use the less-expensive upgrade version of Windows XP Professional to upgrade from Windows 98, Windows Me, Windows NT 4.0, and Windows 2000 to Windows XP Professional.
- You can use the less expensive upgrade version of Windows XP Home Edition to upgrade from Windows 98 or Windows Me to Windows XP Home Edition. (Recall that Windows XP Home Edition uses the same core as Windows XP Professional without some of its features.)
- If you currently have Windows 95 installed, you must do a clean install using the more expensive For a New PC version of Windows XP Professional or Windows XP Home Edition.
- Regardless of whether you have an OS currently installed, you can still choose to do a clean install if you want a fresh start. Unless you erase your hard drive, reformat it, or delete partitions before the upgrade, data on the hard drive is not erased even if you convert to a new file system during the installation. OS settings and installed software will not carry forward into the new installation.

Final Checklist

Before you begin the installation, complete the final checklist shown in Table 21-3 to verify that you are ready to begin.

Table 21-3 Checklist for use before installing Windows XP

Things to Do	Further Information
Does the PC meet the minimum or recommended hardware requirement?	CPU: RAM: Hard drive size: Free space on the hard drive:
Have you run the Readiness Analyzer or checked the Microsoft Web site to verify that all your hardware and software qualify?	List hardware and software that need to be upgraded:
Do you have the product key available?	Product key:
Have you decided how you will join a network?	Workgroup name: Domain name:
Will you do an upgrade or clean install?	Current operating system: Does the old OS qualify for an upgrade?

Table 21-3 Checklist for use before installing Windows XP (continued)

Things to Do	Further Information
Verify that your hard drive is ready.	Size of the hard drive partition: Free space on the partition: File system you plan to use:
For a clean install, will you set up a dual boot?	List reasons for a dual boot: For a dual boot Size of the second partition: Free space on the second partition: File system you plan to use:
Have you backed up important data on your hard drive?	Location of backup:

Installation Process

Follow these general directions to perform a clean install of Windows XP on a PC that does not already have an OS installed:

1. Boot from the Windows XP CD, which displays the menu in Figure 21-3. This menu might change slightly from one Windows XP build to another. If your PC does not boot from a CD, go to a command prompt and enter the command **D:\i386\Winnt.exe**, substituting the drive letter for your CD-ROM drive for D. (The path might vary depending on the release of Windows XP.) The End User License Agreement appears. Accept the agreement.

```
Windows XP Professional Setup
===================== =

    Welcome to Setup.

    This portion of the Setup program prepares Microsoft ( R )
    Windows ( R ) XP to run on your computer.

        •   To set up Windows XP now, press ENTER.

        •   To repair a Windows XP installation using Recovery Console,
            press R.

        •   To quit Setup without installing Windows XP, press F3.

ENTER=Continue  R=RepairF3=Quit
```

Figure 21-3 Windows XP Setup opening menu

2. Setup lists all partitions that it finds on the hard drive, the file system of each partition, and the size of the partition. It also lists any free space on the drive that is not partitioned. From this screen, you can create and delete partitions and select the partition on which you want to install Windows XP. If you plan to have more than one partition on the drive, only create one partition at this time. The partition must be at least 2 GB in size and have 1.5 GB free. After the installation is done, you can use Disk Management to create the other partitions. Figure 21-4 shows an example of the list provided by Setup when the entire hard drive has not yet been partitioned.

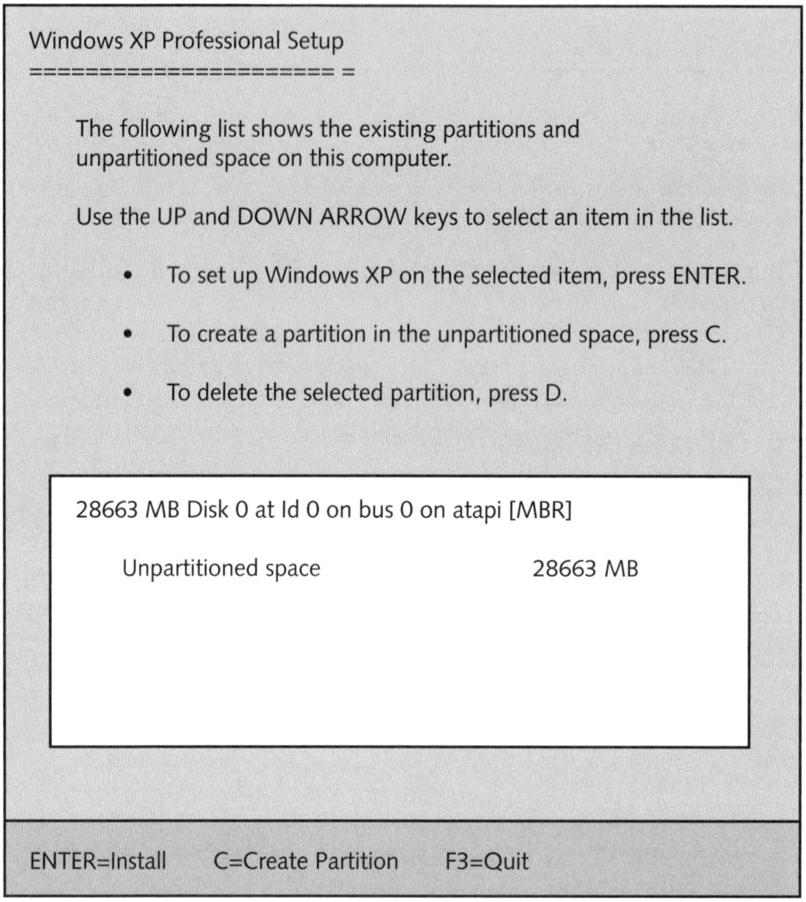

Figure 21-4 During Setup, you can create and delete partitions and select a partition on which to install Windows XP

3. In the previous step, if you created a new partition, Setup asks you which file system you want to use to format the partition, NTFS or FAT. If the partition is at least 2 GB in size, the FAT file system will be FAT32. Select a file system for the partition. The Setup program completes the text-based portion of setup and loads the graphical interface for the rest of the installation. The PC then restarts.

4. Select your geographical location from the list provided, which will be used by Windows XP to decide how to display dates, times, numbers, and currency. Select your keyboard layout. Different keyboards can be used to accommodate special characters for other languages.
5. Enter your name, the name of your organization, and your product key.
6. Enter the computer name and the password for the Administrator account. This password is stored in the security database on this PC. If you are joining a domain, the computer name is the name assigned to this computer by the network administrator managing the domain controller.

TIP

It is *very* important that you not forget the Administrator password. You will not be able to log onto the system without it.

7. Select the date, time, and time zone. The PC will reboot.
8. If you are connected to a network, you will be asked to choose how to configure your network settings, Typical or Custom. The Typical setting installs Client for Microsoft Networks, File and Printer Sharing, and TCP/IP using dynamically assigned IP addresses. The Custom setting allows you to configure the network differently. If you are not sure which to use, use the Typical settings. You can change them later.
9. Enter a workgroup or domain name. If you are joining a domain, the network administrator will have given you specific directions on how to configure user accounts on the domain.

For a clean install on a PC that already has an OS installed, follow these general directions:

1. Close any open applications. Disable any boot management software or antivirus software running.
2. Insert the Windows XP CD in the CD-ROM drive. Autorun launches the opening window shown in Figure 21-5.
3. Select the option to **Install Windows XP**. On the next screen, under Installation Type, select **New Installation**. Read and accept the licensing agreement. The installation process works the same as described above, picking up with Step 3.

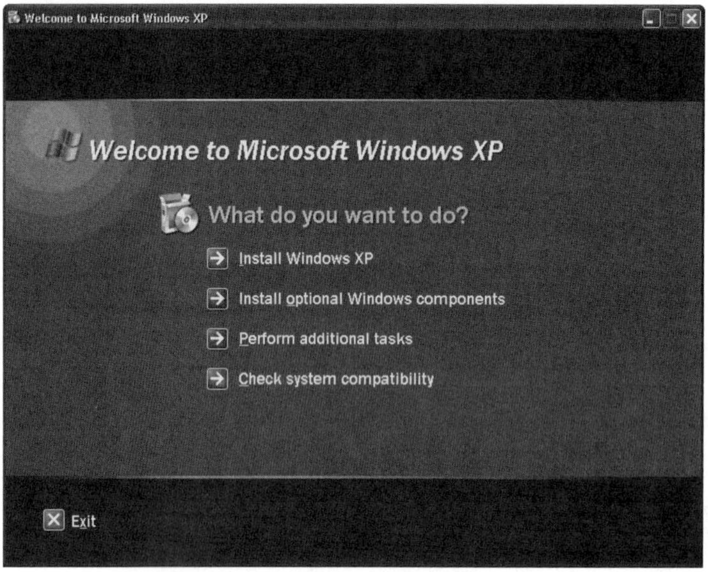

Figure 21-5 Windows XP Setup menu

When performing an upgrade to Windows XP, follow these general directions:

1. Before you begin the installation, do the following to prepare the system:
   - Clean up the hard drive: erase unneeded or temporary files, empty the Recycle Bin, run Disk Defragmenter, and do a ScanDisk of the drive.
   - If you have determined that you must upgrade hardware or software and that these upgrades are compatible with your old OS, perform the upgrades and verify that the hardware or software is working.
   - If you do not have the latest BIOS for your motherboard, flash your BIOS.
   - Back up important files.
   - Scan the hard drive for viruses using a current version of antivirus software.
   - If you have a compressed hard drive, uncompress the drive. The only exception to this is that if you are using Windows NT file compression on an NTFS drive, you do not need to uncompress it.
   - Uninstall any hardware or software that you know will not be compatible with Windows XP and for which you do not have an upgrade available.
2. Insert the Windows XP Upgrade CD in the CD-ROM drive. The Autorun feature should launch the Setup program, with the menu shown in Figure 21-5.
3. If the Setup menu does not appear, you can enter the Setup command in the Run dialog box. Select the option to **Install Windows XP**.

4. On the next screen, under Installation Type, select **Upgrade**. The following menu gives you two options:
   - *Express Upgrade* — This upgrade uses existing Windows folders and uses all existing settings it can.
   - *Custom Upgrade* — This upgrade allows you to change the installation folder and the language options. Using this option, you can also change the file system to NTFS.
5. Select the type of upgrade and accept the licensing agreement.
6. Select the partition on which to install Windows XP. If the drive is configured as FAT and you want to convert to NTFS, you specify that now. Note that Windows XP has an uninstall utility that allows you to revert back to Windows 98 if necessary. This uninstall tool will not work if you convert FAT to NTFS.
7. Setup performs an analysis of the system and reports any problems with compatibility. Stop the installation if the problems indicate that you will not be able to operate the system after the installation.
8. For an upgrade from Windows 98 or Windows Me to Windows XP, the Setup program converts whatever information in the registry it can to Windows XP. At the end of the installation process, you are given the opportunity to join a domain. For Windows NT and Windows 2000 upgrades, almost all registry entries are carried forward into the new OS, and the information about a domain is not requested because it is copied from the old OS into Windows XP.

Upgrading from Windows NT or Windows 2000 to Windows XP is the easiest type of upgrade because these operating systems all have similar registries and support applications and devices in the same way. Nearly all applications that run on Windows NT or Windows 2000 will run on Windows XP. When upgrading from Windows NT to Windows XP, the NTFS file system is automatically converted to the Windows XP version.

TIP

Antivirus software designed to use the Windows NT NTFS file system might not run under the Windows XP NTFS file system because of the way some antivirus programs filter software as it accesses the file system. You might have to upgrade your antivirus software once Windows XP is installed.

Setting Up a Dual Boot

You can configure Windows XP to set up a dual boot with another operating system. Start the installation as you would for a clean install on a PC with another operating system already installed. When given the opportunity, choose to install Windows XP on a different partition than the other OS. Windows XP recognizes that another OS is installed and sets up the Startup menu to offer it as an option for booting. After the installation, when you boot with a dual boot, the Startup menu automatically appears asking you to select an operating system, as shown in Figure 21-6.

```
Please select the operating system to start:

    Microsoft Windows XP Professional
    Microsoft Windows 98

Use the up and down arrow keys to move the highlight to your choice.
Press ENTER to choose.

For troubleshooting and advanced startup options for Windows, press F8.
```

Figure 21-6 Menu displayed for a dual boot

The first active partition (drive C) must be set up with a file system that both operating systems understand. For example, for a dual boot with Windows 98, use the FAT32 or FAT16 file system. For a dual boot with Windows 2000, use either the FAT or the NTFS file system. The other operating system should be installed first, and then you can install Windows XP in a different partition. When you install Windows XP on another active partition or an extended partition, it will place only the files necessary to boot in the first active partition, which it calls the system partition. This causes Windows XP to initiate the boot rather than the other OS. The rest of Windows XP is installed on a second partition, which Windows XP calls the boot partition. This is the same way that Windows NT and Windows 2000 manage a dual boot with an older OS.

TIP: When setting up a dual boot, always install the older operating system first.

Earlier Windows operating systems were not aware of applications installed under the other OS in a dual boot, but Windows XP is. For example, if you set up a dual boot with Windows XP and Windows 98, an application installed under Windows 98 can be executed from Windows XP. This application might be listed under the Start menu of Windows XP. If it is not, you can use Windows XP Explorer to locate the program file. Double-click the application to run it from Windows XP. This makes it easier to implement a dual boot because you don't have to install an application under both OSs.

After the Installation

Immediately after you have installed Windows XP, there are several things to do to activate the OS, prepare the OS for use, and to back up the hard drive in preparation for a disaster. These steps are discussed in this section.

Product Activation

Product activation is a method used by Microsoft to prevent unlicensed use of its software so that you must purchase a Windows XP license for each installation of Windows XP. It was introduced with Microsoft Office XP, and Microsoft has said it will continue it for all future Microsoft products. The first time you log on to the system after the installation is complete, the Activate Windows dialog box appears giving these three options (see Figure 21-7):

- Yes, let's activate Windows over the Internet now
- Yes, I want to telephone a customer service representative to activate Windows
- No, remind me to activate Windows every few days

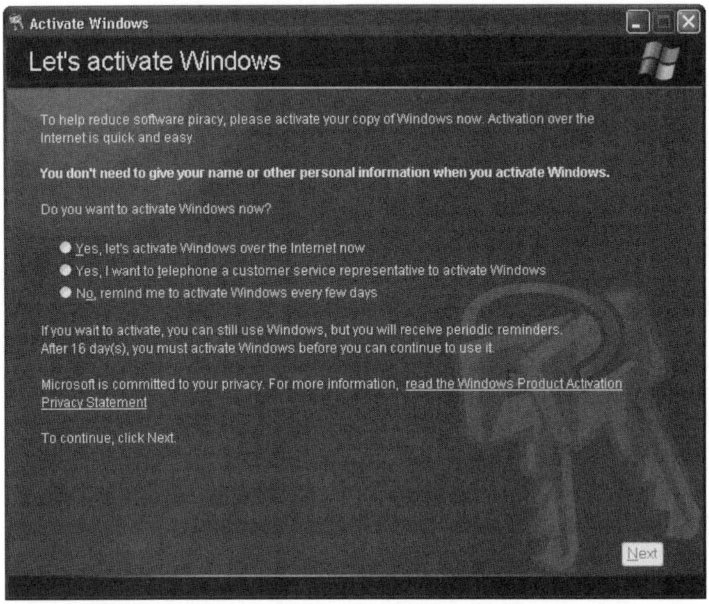

Figure 21-7 Product activation is a strategy used by Microsoft to prevent software piracy

If you choose to activate Windows over the Internet and are connected to the Internet at the time, the process is almost instant. Windows XP sends a numeric identifier to a Microsoft server, which sends a certificate activating the product on your PC. You have up to 30 days after installation to activate Windows XP, after which time the system will refuse to boot. If you install Windows XP from the same CD on a different computer and you attempt to activate Windows from the new PC, a dialog box appears telling you of the suspected violation of the license agreement. You can call a Microsoft operator and explain what caused the discrepancy. If your explanation is reasonable (for example, you uninstalled Windows XP from one PC and installed it on another), the operator can issue you a valid certificate. You can then type the certificate value into a dialog box to complete the boot process.

Transferring User Files and Preferences to a New PC

Windows XP offers a utility that helps you transfer user files and preferences from one computer to another that has just had Windows XP installed. The **User State Migration Tool (USMT)** transfers user files and folders, display properties, taskbar options, and browser and e-mail settings from a Windows 9x or Windows NT/2000/XP computer. This utility can help in making a smooth transition for a user who is moving from one PC to another, without having to copy files and reconfigure OS settings. The process involves these three steps:

1. Use a Windows XP computer to create a disk that contains the Files and Settings Transfer Wizard. This PC does not need to be the same PC that will later receive the transfer.
2. Use the disk on the source computer (the user's old computer) to run the wizard and copy the user state to a server hard drive or removable media such as a Zip drive.
3. On the destination computer (the user's new computer), use the wizard to transfer the user state to this computer.

To begin the process, use the Files and Settings Transfer Wizard to create the disk. To access the wizard, click Start, All Programs, Accessories, System Tools, Files and Settings Transfer Wizard. The wizard launches and the Welcome to the Files and Settings Transfer Wizard window opens. Click Next and the Wizard asks you if this is the New computer or Old computer. Select New computer, and then click Next. Figure 21-8 shows the next screen, on which you can choose to create the disk or declare that you are ready to put the information on the new computer. On the screen, note that you can also use the Windows XP CD to launch the wizard on the old computer rather than creating the disk.

After you have created the disk or chosen to use the Windows XP CD, go to the old computer, launch the wizard, and retrieve the files and settings. Then, return to this screen on the new computer and choose to put the information on the new computer.

Instead of using the wizard, you can also use two commands at the command prompt. Scanstate copies the information to a server or removable media, and Loadstate copies the information to the destination computer. These utilities can be included in batch files and executed automatically when implementing Windows XP over a large number of computers in an enterprise. For details on how to use the command lines in a batch file, see the *Windows XP Resource Kit* by Microsoft Press.

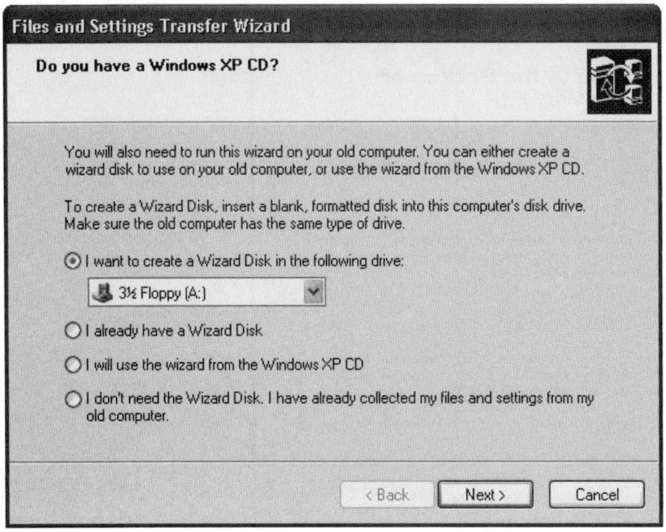

Figure 21-8 The first step in using the Files and Settings Transfer Wizard is to create the Wizard Disk

Preparing for Later Problems with the OS

Once the installation is completed, hardware and software are installed, and user preferences are set, it is a good idea to guard against later problems with the OS by creating a backup of the hard drive. Windows XP offers a utility called the **Automated System Recovery (ASR)** process that allows you to restore an entire hard drive volume or logical drive to its state at the time the backup of the volume was made. This process creates the backup and also creates an ASR floppy disk that allows you to use the backup to recover the system later. You will learn how to recover a failed system using a backup later in this chapter. In this section, you learn how to create the backup.

The backup file created will be just as large as the contents of the hard drive volume, so you will need a massive backup medium such as another partition on this or another local hard drive or file server, a tape drive, or a writable CD-R or CD-RW drive.

CAUTION

Do not back up the logical drive or volume to a folder on the same volume. The ASR backup process allows you to do this, but restoring later from this backup will not work.

Follow these directions to create the backup and the ASR floppy disk:

1. Click **Start**, **All Programs**, **Accessories**, **System Tools**, **Backup**. The Backup and Restore window appears (see Figure 21-9).

Figure 21-9 Use the Backup or Restore utility to back up the hard drive partition once the Windows XP installation is complete

2. Click the **Advanced Mode** link. The Backup Utility window appears. Click **Automated System Recovery Wizard**. On the following screen, click **Next**.
3. The Backup Destination window appears. Select the location of the medium to receive the backup and insert a disk into the floppy disk drive. This disk will become the ASR disk. Click **Next**.
4. Click **Finish**. The backup process shows its progress as seen in Figure 21-10.

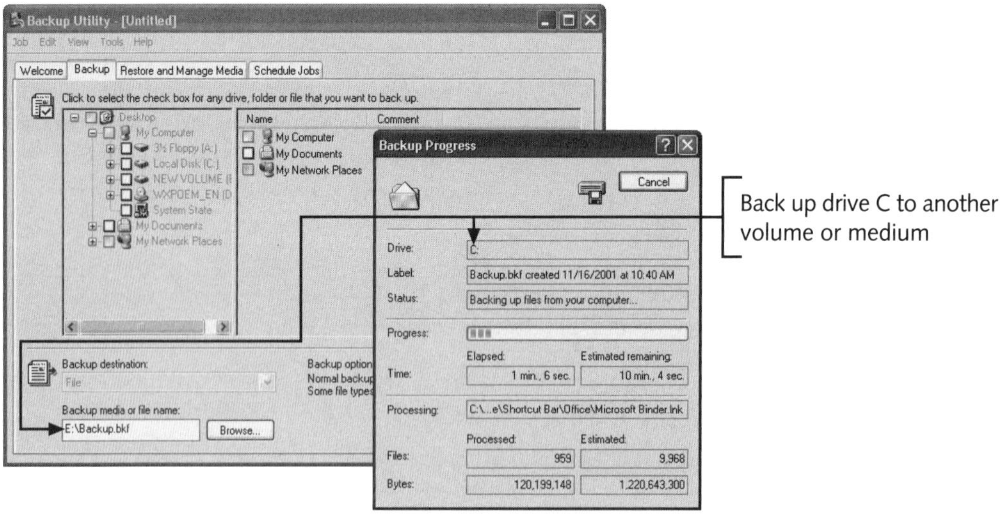

Figure 21-10 The Backup utility can create a backup of drive C and an ASR disk to be used later for the Automated System Recovery

5. When backup is finished, label the ASR disk with the name of the disk, the date it was created, and the computers name, and put it in a safe place.

> TIP Just as with Windows 2000, you can back up the system state. If you back up the system state when you complete an installation, and a failure occurs in the future, you can restore the system state without overwriting user data on the hard drive. This is less drastic than the Automated System Recovery process that restores the entire volume.

USING WINDOWS XP

Now that you have learned how to successfully install Windows XP and guard the system against a potential failure, let's take a closer look at how it works and what it can do. One difference you will note immediately on using Windows XP for the first time is the desktop, seen in Figure 21-11. When the OS is first installed, the Recycle Bin is the only shortcut on the desktop. Also note that the Start menu is organized with a more graphical look. Notice in Figure 21-11 that the username for the person currently logged on shows at the top of the Start menu. Applications at the top of the Start menu are said to be "pinned" to the Start menu and are permanently listed there until you change them in a Start menu setting. Applications that are used often are listed below the pinned applications and can change from time to time. The programs in the white column of the Start menu on the left side are user-oriented, and the programs on the dark column on the right side of the menu are OS-oriented.

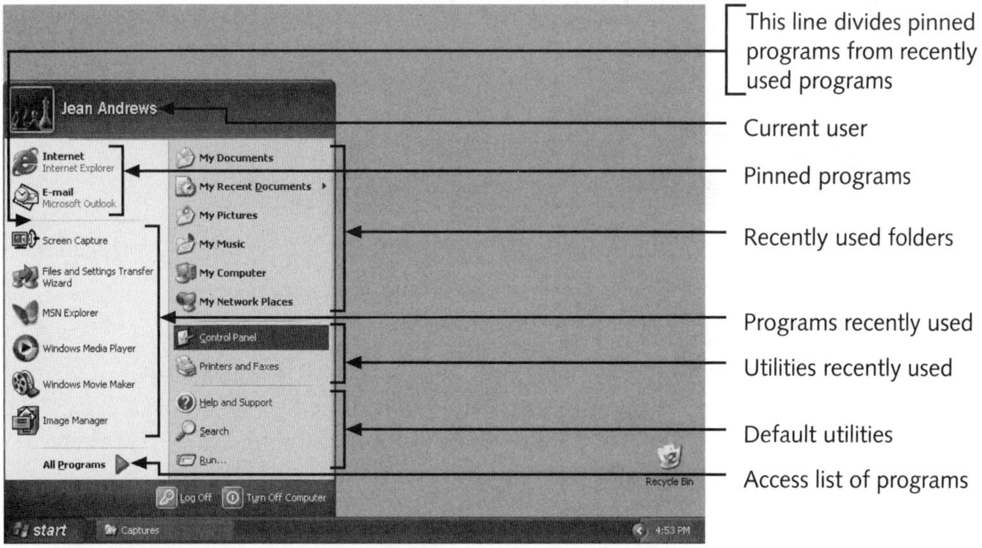

Figure 21-11 The Windows XP desktop and Start menu

When you click All Programs, the list of currently installed software appears as it does for Windows 2000. Figure 21-12 shows the default entries under Accessories, System Tools. You have already seen two of these, Backup and Files and Settings Transfer Wizard. Also, after Windows is installed, you can use the Activate Windows option on this menu to activate Windows XP. You will learn about several other options on this menu later in the chapter.

When you drill down to windows and menus on these windows, you will notice you have more control over how and where things are displayed. Overall, if you are familiar with Windows 2000, learning to use Windows XP is easy and intuitive. One example of how you can change the way a window appears is through the Control Panel. To access the Control Panel, click Start, All Programs, and Control Panel. Figure 21-13 shows the Control Panel in Category View. Select a category in order to see the applets in that category, or click Switch to Classic View to see the applets when you first open the Control Panel as you did with earlier versions of Windows.

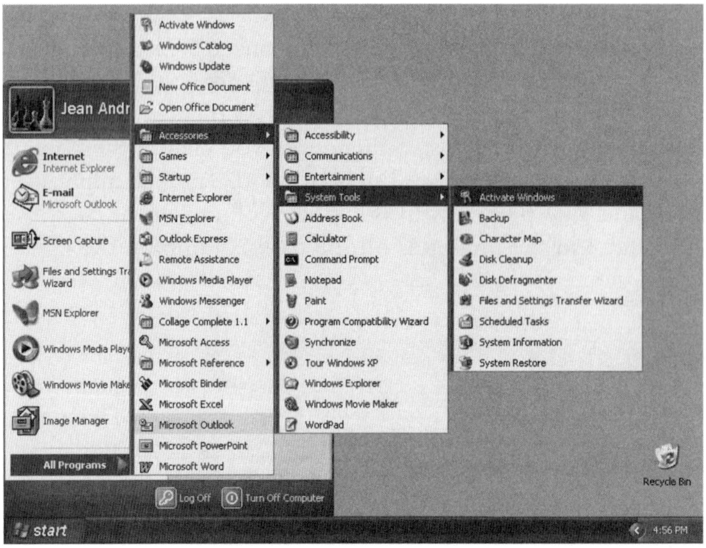

Figure 21-12 Click Start, All Programs to view the list of currently installed software

Customizing the Windows XP Desktop

There are several things you can do to customize the Windows XP desktop. For example, you can change the background on the desktop (called the wallpaper), create shortcuts, and control what goes in the system tray. This section looks at each of these ways to make the desktop look and work the way you want it to.

> TIP
>
> Each user account has a different desktop configuration, so if you want to create a customized desktop for a user, you must first log on to the system under that user account.

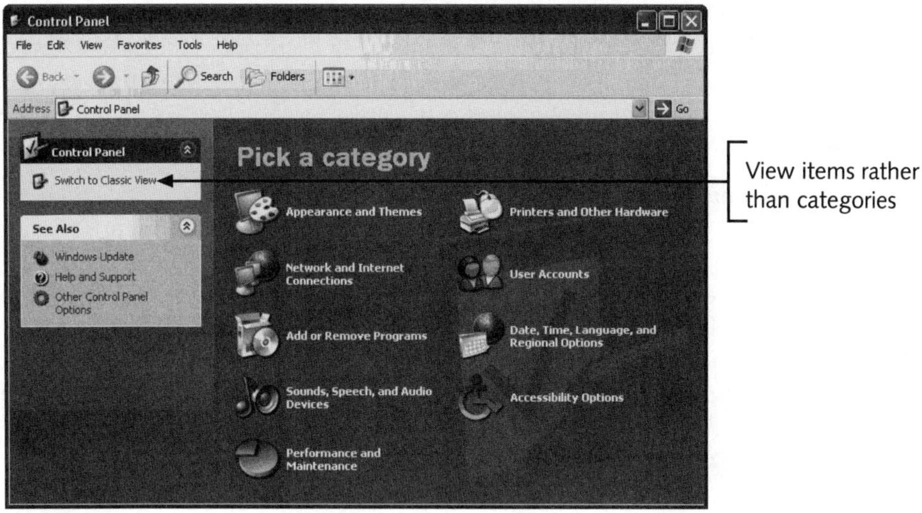

Figure 21-13 The Control Panel is organized by category although you can easily switch to the Classic View

Managing Shortcuts

When you first install Windows XP, by default, only the Recycle Bin shows on the desktop. To add other shortcuts that normally were on the Windows 2000 desktop, right-click anywhere on the desktop and select Properties from the shortcut menu. (You can also select the Display icon in Control Panel.) The Display Properties window appears (see Figure 21-14). Click the Desktop tab.

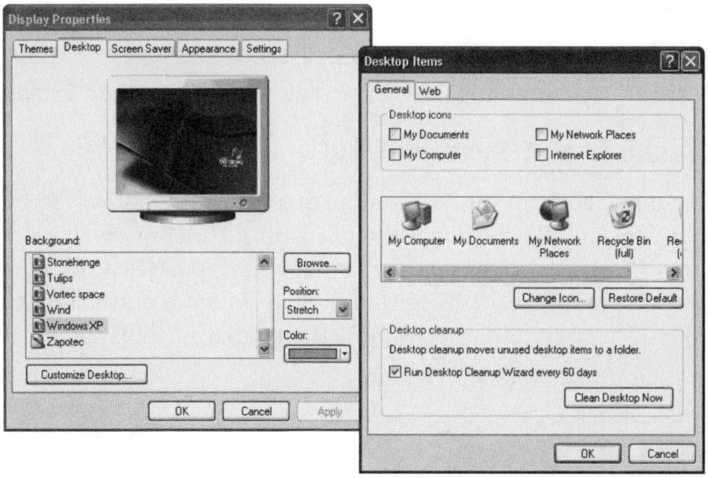

Figure 21-14 Managing the Windows XP desktop

Click Customize Desktop to display the Desktop Items window, also shown in Figure 21-14. You can check My Documents, My Computer, My Network Places, and Internet Explorer to add these icons to the desktop. Also notice on this window the option to have Windows clean up your desktop by moving any shortcuts that you have not used in the last 60 days to a separate folder.

You can add a program shortcut to the desktop by right-clicking a program name in the Start, All Programs list and then selecting Copy from the Shortcut menu. Then, right-click anywhere on the desktop and select Paste from the shortcut menu. A shortcut is created and placed on the desktop. You can also use Windows Explorer to create a shortcut. From Explorer, right-click a program filename or the filename of a document or data file, and then select Create Shortcut from the shortcut menu (see Figure 21-15). Then, drag the shortcut created to the desktop.

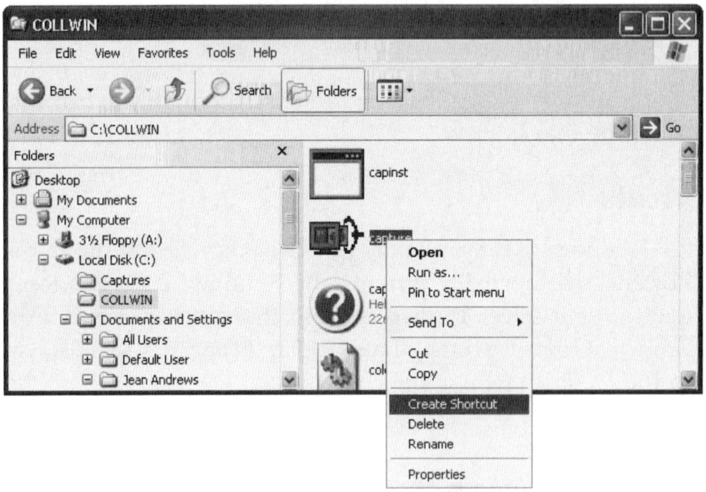

Figure 21-15 Create a shortcut to a file using the file's shortcut menu in Explorer

Windows XP Taskbar and System Tray

The taskbar can be controlled from the Taskbar and Start Menu windows. Access the windows by using the Taskbar and Start Menu icon in Control Panel or by right-clicking the taskbar and selecting Properties. Either way, the window in Figure 21-16 appears. From it you can add items to and remove items from the Start Menu, control how the taskbar manages items in the system tray, and specify how the taskbar is displayed.

You might want to display frequently used programs as icons in the taskbar. To do that, right-click the taskbar, select Toolbars, and then click Quick Launch. Also, the system tray can sometimes get cluttered with several icons for running services such as the volume control and network connectivity. Windows XP automatically hides these icons. When they are hidden, to unhide them, click the left arrow on the right side of the taskbar. In addition, by using the options available on the taskbar shortcut menu, you can add programs to the Quick Launch toolbar, customize the taskbar properties, and add new toolbars to the taskbar.

Managing Audio and Video

Windows XP has several built-in features to manage video and audio, including support for inputting images from digital cameras and scanners, a Windows Movie Maker for editing video and Windows Media Player, Version 8. (Windows Me has Media Player, Version 7.) With Media Player you can play DVDs, CDs, and Internet radio. There's a jukebox for organizing audio files, including MP3 files used on music CDs. You can also burn your own music CDs using Media Player with a CD-R or CD-RW drive. To access the Media Player, click Start, All Programs, Windows Media Player. Figure 21-17 shows the Media Player window.

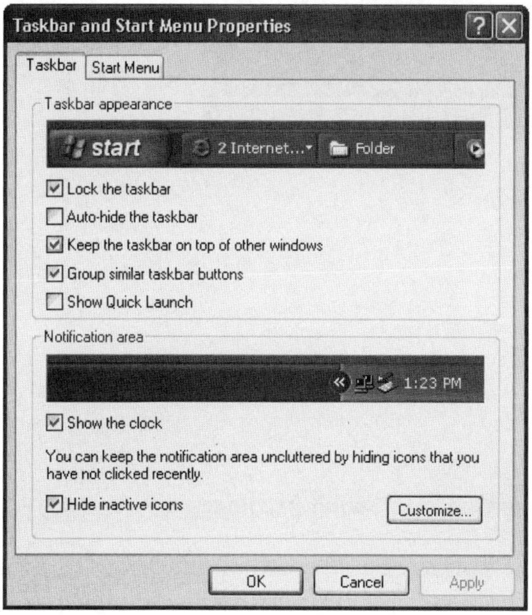

Figure 21-16 Use the Taskbar and Start Menu Properties window to control what is displayed in the Start menu and taskbar

Just as with older versions of Windows, you can record and manage sound from the Entertainment group of Windows and manage sounds for Windows events from the sound applet in Control Panel. To record sound, if you have a microphone connected to a sound card, click Start, All Programs, Accessories, Entertainment, and Sound Recorder. The Sound Recorder appears, as shown in Figure 21-18. Click the Record button (red dot in lower right corner) to record a sound, such as your own voice, into a sound file. There are several types of sound files, including MP3 files (with .mp3 file extension), used on audio CDs, and Wave files (with .wav file extension). Windows uses .wav files to record sound. Later, you can substitute this .wav file for one of the Windows sounds that is played when you open or close applications, shut down Windows, or perform many other Windows activities that can be accompanied by sound. To change the sounds for various Windows events, from Control Panel, open the Sounds and Audio Devices applet, and select the Sounds tab.

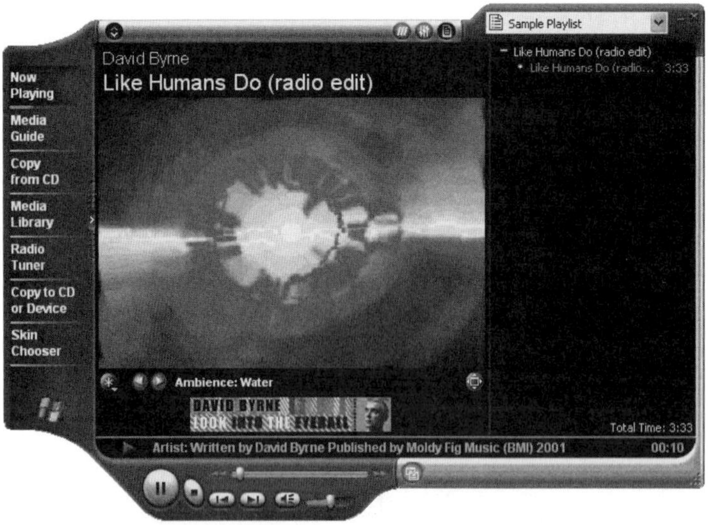

Figure 21-17 Windows Media Player

Figure 21-18 Record sounds using Windows Sound Recorder

Media Player has its own volume control, but there is another way to adjust sound. From the Control Panel, open the Sounds and Audio Devices applet and select the Volume tab. If you check Place volume icon in the taskbar, you can easily adjust the sound from the taskbar.

> TIP: Two ways to control sound volume are to use the Windows controls or use the manual controls on an amplifier or speaker.

Multiple Logins and Remote Assistance

Windows XP allows more than one user to be logged in at the same time. To switch from one account to another, click Start, Logoff. The Log Off Windows dialog box opens, giving you two choices: Switch User and Log Off. Click Switch User, and then select a new account form the list of user accounts. After you have entered a password, the screen will go blank and then the desktop configured for the new user appears. Each user can have his or her own set of applications open at the same time. When users switch back and forth, Windows keeps separate instances of applications open for each user.

Windows XP also offers a new feature called **Remote Assistance**. Using this utility, a user sitting at the PC can give a support technician at a remote location full access to the desktop so the technician can use the desktop just as she would if sitting in front of the PC. This is useful when the user is inexperienced and is having trouble following the technician's directions as the technician is investigating and troubleshooting problems with Windows XP.

There are three stages in using Remote Assistance in Windows XP:

1. The user on the host computer must send an invitation by clicking **Start**, **Help and Support**, **Ask for Assistance**, **Invite a friend to connect to your computer with Remote Assistance**, and **Invite Someone to Help You**.
2. The remote user (the helper) responds to the host user's request.
3. The host user accepts the remote user's assistance. When the remote user accepts the request for help, the Remote Assistance dialog box appears on the host computer, and the host user clicks Yes to enable the remote user to view the host computer screen and to send instant messages.

INSTALLING HARDWARE AND APPLICATIONS

In this section, you will learn how to install hardware and applications, and you will also learn several ways to solve problems with both. Later in the chapter, you will learn about more tools and procedures you can use to troubleshoot a failed system, program, or hardware device. We will first look at how to install hardware.

Installing Hardware

Since Windows XP is relatively new to the market, a device might not come with a Windows XP-compatible driver. To see if a hardware device has a driver that is known to be compatible with Windows XP, see the Microsoft Web site *windowsupdate.microsoft.com*. Download the latest driver from the Microsoft Web site or the Web site of the device manufacturer. Windows XP offers three processes that can help with solving problems with devices:

- Verifying that the driver is certified by Microsoft
- Providing a way to automatically find an update for a driver
- Rolling back a driver in case an updated driver fails

Just as with earlier Windows operating systems, when Windows XP is first started, if it senses a new device is present, it automatically launches the Found New Hardware Wizard, which gives you two options:

- Install the software automatically (Recommended)
- Install from a list or specific location (Advanced)

Select the option to Install the Software automatically, and then click Next. During the installation process, you are given the opportunity to click Have Disk to provide a driver supplied by the manufacturer, rather than selecting the device from a list, which results in using a Windows driver. First attempt to use the Windows XP driver. If it causes problems, search both the Microsoft Web site and the manufacturer's Web site for the latest updated driver. If the wizard does not automatically launch when you start Windows, you can start it using the Add Hardware icon in Control Panel.

Using Device Manager

After a device is installed, you can use Device Manager to verify that Windows XP sees no problems with the device. There is more than one way to access Device Manager. One way is to click Start, right-click My Computer, and then select Manage from the shortcut menu. The Computer Management window appears (see Figure 21-19). This powerful tool offers several important utilities to support Windows XP that function the same as they did with Windows 2000. For example, under System Tools, click Device Manager to view it. With Device Manager selected, use the View menu to control how you view devices and resources in Device Manager, similarly to previous versions of Windows. Another way to access Device Manager is to open the System applet in Control Panel, select the Hardware tab, and click Device Manager.

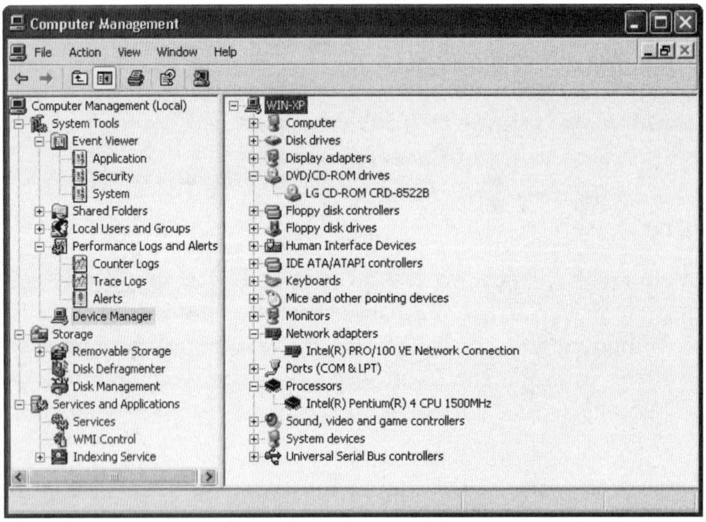

Figure 21-19 Device Manager is one tool available in the Computer Management window

Using Device Manager, you can verify that there are no resource conflicts with the device and that it is working properly as viewed by Windows XP. From Device Manager, Windows XP offers a way to update a driver using the Update Device Driver Wizard. Right-click on a device and select Properties from the shortcut menu. The Properties window for that device appears (see Figure 21-20). Select the Driver tab and click Update Driver... to launch the wizard and follow directions on the screen. The wizard goes to the Microsoft Web site, searches for updates to the driver, informs you if there is an update, and asks permission to install the update. Windows XP will only suggest an update if the hardware ID of the device is an exact match to the hardware ID of the update. A hardware ID is a number assigned to a device by the manufacturer that uniquely identifies the product.

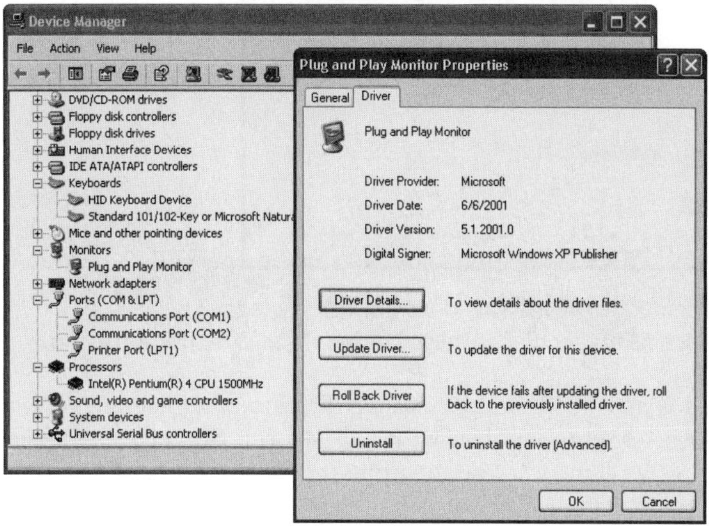

Figure 21-20 Use the Properties window for a device to obtain an updated driver from the Microsoft Web site

> **TIP** If you do not have an always-on connection to the Internet, first connect to the Internet before you launch the Update Device Driver Wizard.

If you update a driver and the new driver does not perform as expected, you can revert to the old driver by using the Driver Rollback feature. To revert to a previous driver, from the Properties window for the device (see Figure 21-20), click Roll Back Driver. If a previous driver is available, it will be installed. In many cases, when a driver is updated, Windows saves the old driver in case you want to revert to it. Note that Windows does not save printer drivers when they are updated and also does not save any drivers if they are not functioning properly at the time of an update.

You can also copy an older driver from another PC or a backup medium to this PC for a rollback. Two files are needed: a .sys file and an .inf file. The .sys file is the actual driver, and the .inf file contains information about the driver. Put these files in the %systemroot%\system32\reinstallbackups\ folder, and then perform the rollback.

TIP: By default, Device Manager does not show legacy devices that are not Plug and Play. To view legacy devices that are installed, on the View menu of Device Manager, check Show hidden devices (see Figure 21-21).

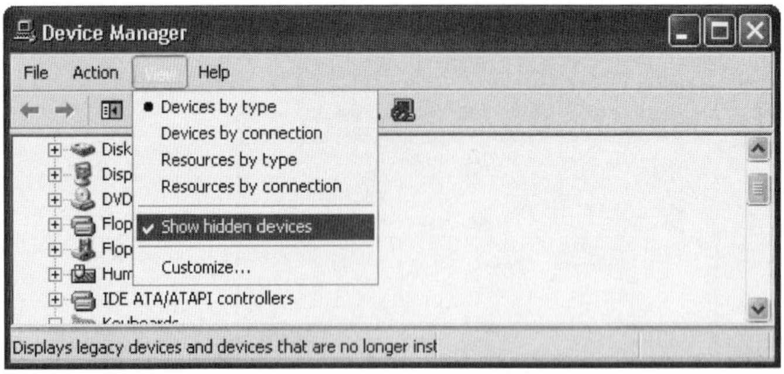

Figure 21-21 By default, Windows XP does not display legacy devices in Device Manager. Show these hidden devices by using the View menu

Windows 2000 and Windows XP support the verification of digital signatures assigned to device drivers. If you suspect a problem with a driver, run **Sigverif.exe** to scan for drivers that are not digitally signed. To use the utility, enter the command in the Run dialog box. Also, during an installation, you can control how Windows handles a driver not digitally signed by using the Hardware tab of the System Properties window.

Installing Applications

Applications are installed under Windows XP as they are under other Windows OSs. You can use the Add or Remove Programs icon in Control Panel, or you can run the application's setup program from the Run dialog box. You can only install software if you have Administrator privileges. An installed program is normally made available to every user when they log on. If a program is not available to all users, try installing the program files in the Documents and Settings\All Users folder.

TIP: You can cause a program to automatically launch each time you start Windows by putting a shortcut to the program in the Startup menu folder for the user. For each user, this folder is Documents and Settings*Username*\Start Menu\Programs\Startup. If you want the software to automatically startup for all users, put the shortcut in this folder: Documents and Settings\All Users\Start Menu\Programs\Startup.

Software is uninstalled using the Add and Remove Programs applet in Control Panel. Open the applet and select the software to uninstall (see Figure 21-22). Then click the Change/Remove icon. If other users are logged on to the system, the Warning message in Figure 21-22 appears. Log everyone off, and then uninstall the software.

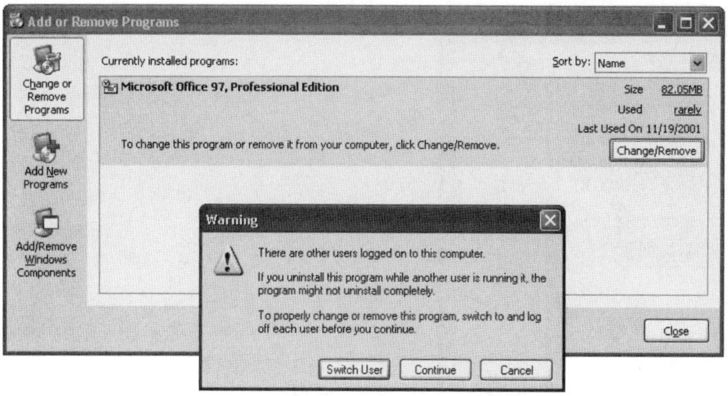

Figure 21-22 To uninstall software using the Add or Remove Programs applet only one user should be logged on to the system

Installing Legacy Software

DOS and Windows 9x applications that would not work under Windows NT and Windows 2000 are more likely to work under Windows XP. Some legacy applications that you should not attempt to run under Windows XP are older versions of antivirus software, and maintenance and cleanup utilities. In these cases, it is best to upgrade your software to versions that are designed to work under Windows XP.

If a legacy application does not start up and run successfully after you have installed it, try the following:

- Check the Microsoft Web site for updates to Windows XP or the Microsoft application (*windowsupdates.microsoft.com*).
- Check the software manufacturer's Web site for updates or suggestions as to how to run the software under Windows XP.
- Consider upgrading the software to a later version.
- Use the Windows XP Compatibility Mode utility.

The **Compatibility Mode** utility provides an application with the environment it expects from the operating system it was designed for, including Windows 95, Windows 98, Windows Me, Windows NT, and Windows 2000. (Compatibility mode does not apply to DOS applications.) There is more than one way to use the utility, but the easiest way is to create a shortcut on the desktop to an installed application and then set the properties of the shortcut to use compatibility mode. After you have created the shortcut to the application, right-click it and select Properties from the shortcut menu. The Properties window displays (see Figure 21-23). Select the Compatibility tab. Check *Run this program in compatibility mode for* and then select the operating system that you want Windows XP to emulate. Click Apply to apply the change. Run the software to find out whether the problem is solved.

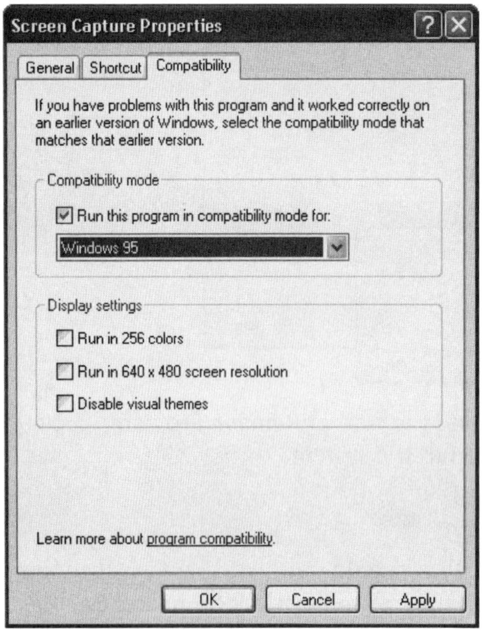

Figure 21-23 Setting Windows XP to run a legacy program in compatibility mode

If it is not solved, if you like, you can provide Microsoft with information that might help it fix the problem in some future Windows XP update. To provide the information, run the Program Compatibility Wizard. Click Start, All Programs, Accessories, Program Compatibility Wizard. Follow directions on the wizard screen to locate the program file. After you locate the program file, you are asked to test the application and then respond to the questions showing in Figure 21-24.

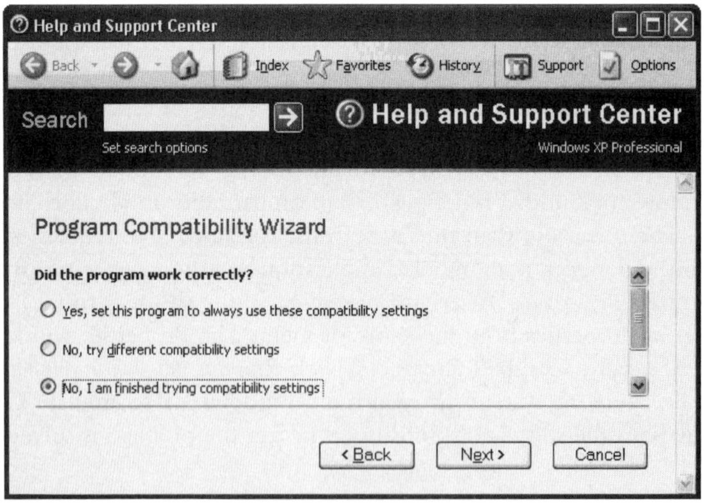

Figure 21-24 Using the Program Compatibility Wizard

If you answer, "No, I am finished trying compatibility settings," then the screen in Figure 21-25 appears. If you respond Yes to the question, "Would you like to send this information to Microsoft?" then the information needed to help Microsoft solve problems with the application will be transmitted to the Microsoft Web site over the Internet.

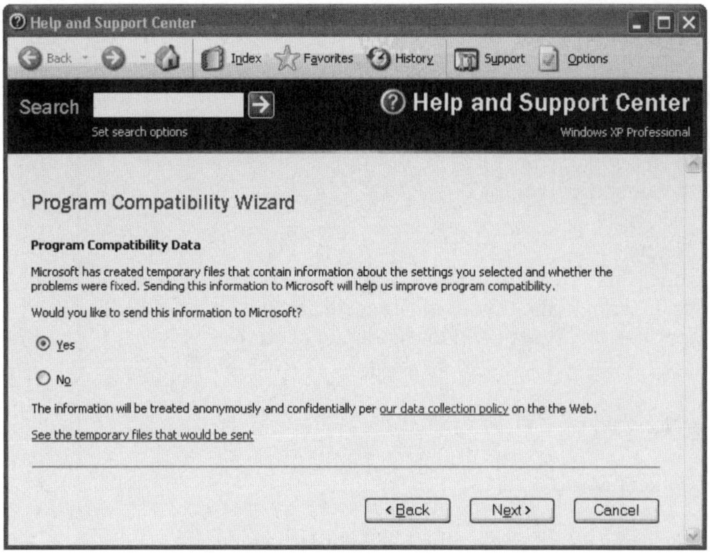

Figure 21-25 If running a legacy program in compatibility mode does not solve the problem, you can send helpful information to Microsoft

TROUBLESHOOTING THE BOOT PROCESS

The Windows XP boot process works the same way as the Windows NT and Windows 2000 boot process. Many of the tools to recover from a failed Windows 2000 boot also work under Windows XP. In addition, Windows XP has added two tools for solving problems with the boot process: System Restore and Automated System Recovery. The tools to use when troubleshooting a failed boot are listed below in the order you should use them. Each tool discussed is more drastic than the one before it, affecting more of the system, installed hardware and software, and user data.

- Last Known Good Configuration and, in certain situations, Driver Rollback
- Safe mode from the Advanced Options menu
- System Restore
- Recovery Console
- Automated System Recovery
- Reinstall Windows XP using the Windows XP CD

The Last Known Good Configuration is the same as under Windows NT and Windows 2000. In addition, you can use Driver Rollback discussed earlier in this guide if you suspect that a single device driver is the source of the problem. The Windows XP Advanced Options menu, shown in Figure 21-26, is also similar to that of Windows 2000. Try Safe Mode with Networking first. If that doesn't work, try Safe Mode.

```
Windows Advanced Options Menu
Please select an option:

    Safe Mode
    Safe Mode with Networking
    Safe Mode with Command Prompt

    Enable Boot Logging
    Enable VGA Mode
    Last Known Good Configuration (your most recent settings that worked)
    Directory Services Restore Mode (Windows domain controllers only)
    Debugging Mode

    Start Windows Normally
    Reboot
    Return to OS Choices Menu

Use the up and down arrow keys to move the highlight to your choice.
```

Figure 21-26 Windows XP Advanced Options menu

> TIP: To access the Advanced Options menu, press F8 while Windows is loading.

The next tool to use if these don't work is System Restore, a tool new to Windows XP, which is discussed next. If that doesn't work, then try the Recovery Console. Commands for the Recovery Console for Windows XP are the same as for Windows 2000. If the Recovery Console fails, then use the Automated System Recovery process to restore the hard drive to its state as of the last ASR backup. If you don't have an ASR backup, then your only recourse is to reinstall Windows XP following directions given earlier in the chapter. Be sure to scan for viruses before you reinstall.

System Restore

The **System Restore** utility is new to Windows XP. It is similar to ScanReg used on previous versions of Windows, but which is not a part of Windows XP; however, System Restore cannot be executed from a command prompt. If you can load Windows XP, then you can use

System Restore to restore the system state to its condition at the time a snapshot was taken of the system settings and configuration. The restore process does not affect user data on the hard drive but can affect installed software and hardware, user settings, and OS configuration settings. The restoration is taken from a snapshot of the system state that was created earlier called a **restore point**. The system automatically creates a restore point before you install new software or hardware or make other changes to the system. You can also manually create a restore point at any time. To create a restore point, do the following:

1. Click **Start**, **All Programs**, **Accessories**, **System Tools**, and **System Restore**. The System Restore window appears.
2. The System Restore window gives you two choices: Restore my computer to an earlier time and Create a restore point. Select **Create a restore point**, and then click **Next**.
3. Type a description of the restore point such as "Just before I updated the video driver." The system automatically assigns the current date and time to the restore point.
4. Click **Create** and then **Close**. The restore point is saved.

Before using System Restore to undo a change, if the change was made to a hardware device, first try Driver Rollback so that as few changes as possible to the system are lost. If Driver Rollback does not work or is not appropriate, do the following to revert the system back to the restore point:

1. Click **Start**, **All Programs**, **Accessories**, **System Tools**, and **System Restore**.
2. Click **Restore my computer to an earlier time**, and then click **Next**. A window appears as shown in Figure 21-27. Notice in the figure that there are two restore points, one created by the system and one created manually.
3. Select the date and time and the specific restore point. Click **Next** twice.

Windows XP will reboot and restore the system state to the settings saved in the restore point. Changes to user data will not be affected but any installation or configuration changes made after the restore point are lost.

When selecting a restore point, select a point as close to the present as you can so that as few changes to the system as possible are lost. If System Restore does not work, try booting into safe mode and using it there. When you select Safe Mode from the Advanced Options menu, Windows XP asks if you want to go directly to System Restore rather than to safe mode. If safe mode does not work, then try going directly to System Restore.

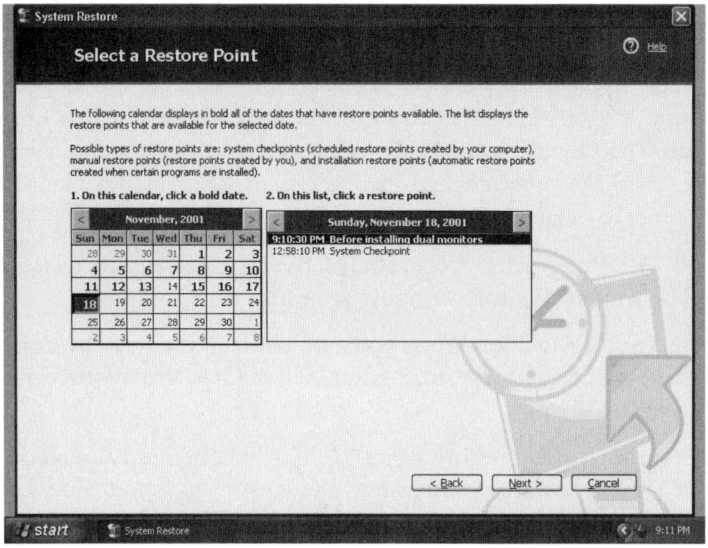

Figure 21-27 Restore points are automatically created daily and every time software or hardware is installed

> **TIP** The main difference between System Restore and Automated System Recovery is that System Restore does not affect user data on the hard drive, but Automated System Recovery does. In order to make it possible to recover a failed system without destroying data, make it a habit to always create a restore point every time you make a change to the system.

Windows XP Startup Disk

Using Windows Explorer, you can create an MS-DOS startup disk that can be used to boot into MS-DOS mode giving you an A prompt. If the hard drive is not protected by some security measure such as NTFS with password protection, then you can access the drive and recover data files. You cannot launch Windows XP using the startup disk or use it to recover from a failed installation. To create a startup disk, using Windows Explorer, right-click on drive A and select Format from the shortcut menu. The Format window opens, as shown in Figure 21-28. Check Create an MS-DOS startup disk, and then click Start. The unhidden files put on the startup disk are shown in the Explorer window in Figure 21-29. In addition to these files, Autoexec.bat, Config.sys, and the Windows 98 versions of Io.sys and Msdos.sys are also placed on the disk as hidden files.

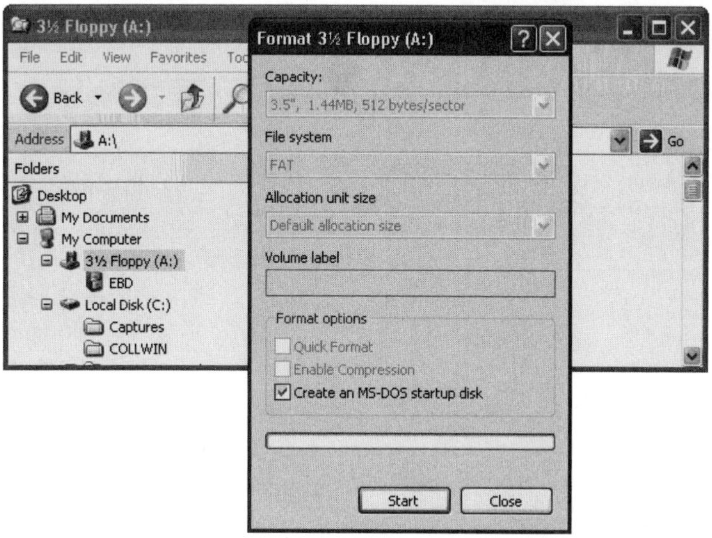

Figure 21-28 Windows XP gives you the ability to create an MS-DOS startup disk

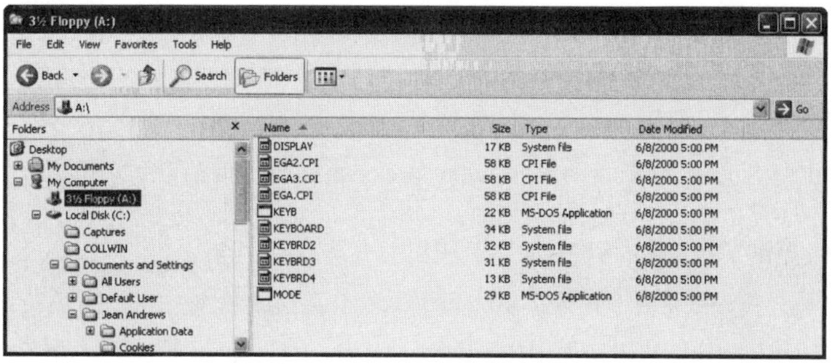

Figure 21-29 Files on the MS-DOS startup disk created by Windows XP

Automated System Recovery

After you finished the Windows XP installation, if you created the Automated System Recovery disk set of the installation, you can use this or a later set of the recovery disks to restore the system partition to its state when the backup was made. You will lose any changes made to the volume or logical drive holding Windows XP since the backup. Everything on the volume since the ASR backup and disk were made is lost, including software and device drivers installed, user data, and any changes to the system configuration. For this reason, it's a good idea to periodically make fresh copies of the ASR disk set. You learned how to make this backup and disk earlier in this chapter.

To revert the hard drive to its state when the last ASR disk set was made, do the following:

1. Insert the Windows XP CD in the CD-ROM drive and hard boot the PC.
2. A message says, "Press any key to boot from CD." Press any key.

3. A blue screen appears with the message, "Press F6 to load RAID or SCSI drivers." If your system uses RAID or SCSI, press **F6**.
4. At the bottom of the blue screen, a message says, "Press F2 to run the Automated System Recovery process." Press **F2**.
5. The screen shown in Figure 21-30 displays, instructing you to insert the ASR floppy disk. Insert the disk, and then press **Enter**.

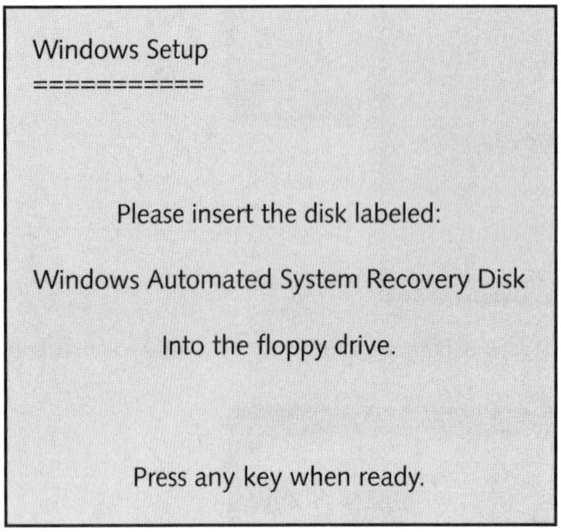

Figure 21-30 The Automatic System Recovery process must have the ASR floppy disk

6. Windows XP Setup does the following:
   - Loads files it needs to run
   - Repartitions and reformats the drive
   - Installs Windows from the Windows XP CD
   - Launches the Automatic System Recovery Wizard to restore the Windows system state, applications and data as it was at the time the last ASR backup was made

The ASR recovery process erases everything on the volume being restored. Figure 21-31 shows one of the above steps in the recovery process, in which you reformat the logical drive just before the Windows XP installation process begins.

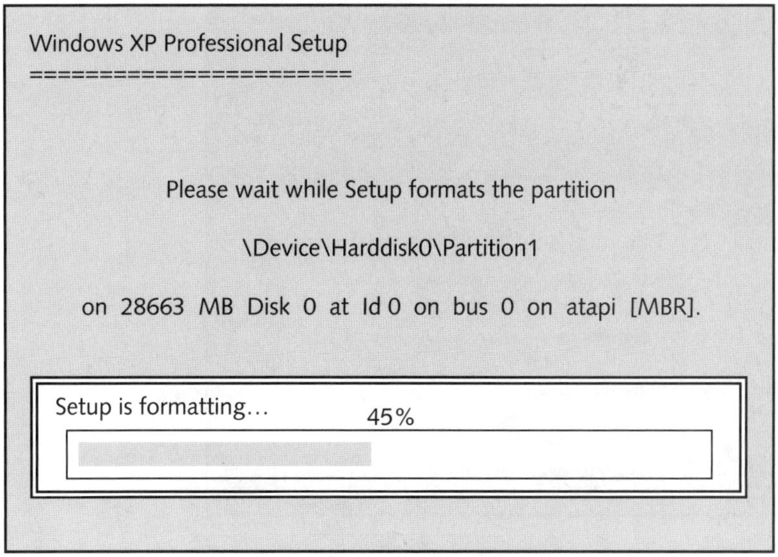

Figure 21-31 As part of the Automatic System Recovery process, Windows XP Setup repartitions and reformats the volume holding Windows XP

Other Maintenance and Troubleshooting Tools

This section discusses other commonly used tools that Windows XP provides for maintenance and troubleshooting. As with the tools for system recovery, some are new or changed in Windows XP, and some operate the same way as they did under Windows 2000.

Windows Update

Windows XP has an automated way to update the OS, applications, and device drivers made available on the Microsoft Web site. Do the following to perform an update. If no user interaction is required, anyone can perform the update, but if decisions must be made during the update, only someone with administrator privileges can perform the update. To do an update including updating the OS, software and drivers, click Start, All Programs, and Windows Update. The Update Wizard takes you to the Microsoft Windows Update Web site (see Figure 21-32). Click Scan for updates and follow the directions on screen. This update process includes updating drivers, a process that can also be started from Device Manager, as you learned earlier in this chapter.

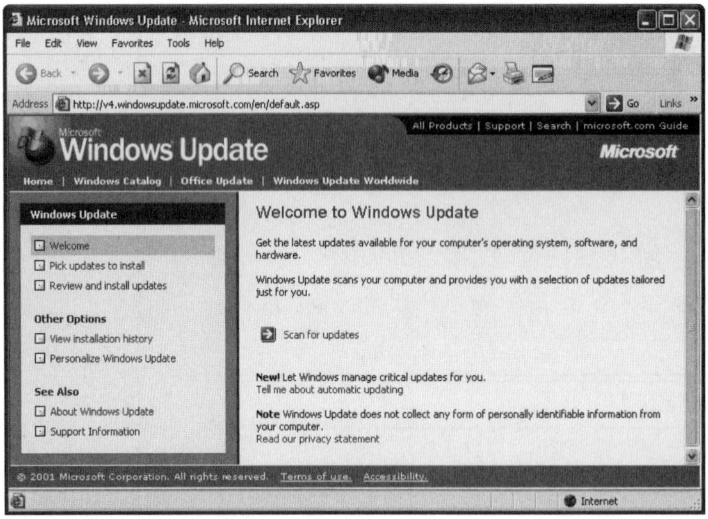

Figure 21-32 The Windows Update utility manages the process of downloading updates from the Microsoft Web site

If there is an update available for your computer, a screen similar to that shown in Figure 21-33 will appear. Note in the figure that the update process found one critical update, nine updates to Windows XP that it does not consider to be critical, and no updates for drivers. To view information about these updates, click on them. In this example, the Critical Update was designed to solve a problem with security, and the nine noncritical updates were about running Java applets, connecting to a UPS (uninterruptible power supply) service, using a CD burner, running legacy applications using compatibility mode, problems with the Files and Settings Transfer Wizard, problems using Remote Assistance across a firewall, and problems with Windows Messenger and Movie Maker. By default, only the critical update is selected for installing. If you want to install the noncritical updates, select the update and then click Add. After you have selected what to update, click *Review and install updates* and follow directions on the screen.

Dr. Watson

Like earlier versions of Windows, Windows XP includes the Dr. Watson utility (Drwatson.exe) to help debug application errors. Dr. Watson is designed to detect problems that applications cause and stop them before the problems affect other applications. This utility records information about application errors in a file called **Drwatson.log**. Note that this is different from the name of the Dr. Watson log file in Windows 2000 (Drwtsn32.log).

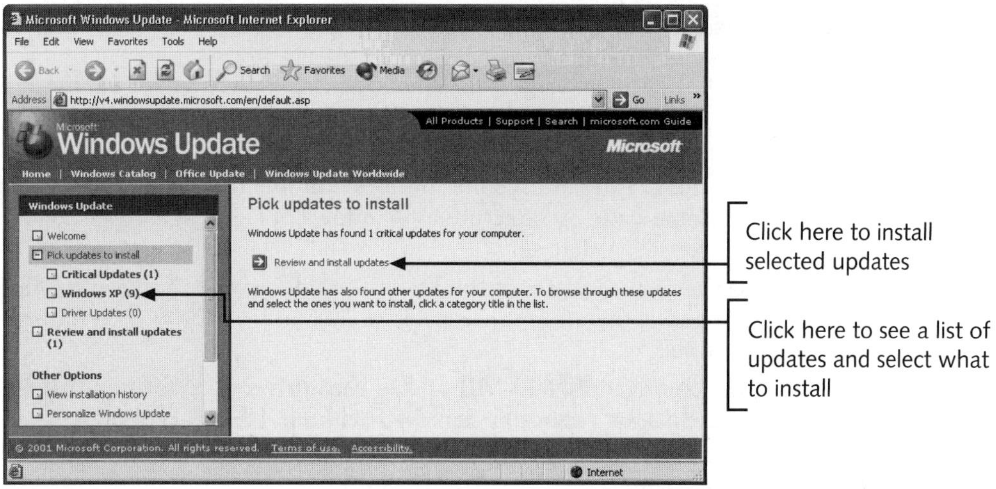

Figure 21-33 Windows Update process found updates appropriate to this computer

Registry Editor

Another utility that Windows includes for maintenance and troubleshooting is the Registry Editor. Windows 2000 included two versions of this utility: Regedit.exe and Regedit32.exe. Windows XP includes only one, Regedit.exe, but allows you to access it using either name. As with Windows 2000, to access the Registry Editor, click Start, Run and type in regedit.exe (or regedit32.exe), and then click OK. You can use the Registry Editor to back up, edit, or restore the registry.

CAUTION

Remember that you should not manually edit the registry unless absolutely necessary, because mistakes in the registry can have drastic consequences for your system. Also, using the Backup utility, you can back up the system state just as with Windows 2000. Always back up the system state before editing the registry.

Administrative Tools

The tools under Administrative Tools, including Event Viewer, Performance Monitor, and Computer Management that were available with Windows 2000, work much the same in Windows XP. Windows 2000 Computer Management tools, including Event Viewer, Disk Management, Performance Logs and Alerts, and Disk Defragmenter are also found in the Windows XP Computer Management console.

Chapter Summary

- There are presently three versions of Windows XP: Windows XP Home Edition, Windows XP Professional, and Windows XP 64-bit Edition.
- Though the Windows XP interface looks different from that of earlier versions of Windows and the OS organizes some utilities and functions differently, Windows XP is built on the same basic architecture as Windows NT and Windows 2000 and has the same basic kernel structure.
- Windows XP has solved many of the known problems with Windows 2000 that caused crashes and is therefore more stable than Windows 2000 or Windows NT. It is also easier to install.
- Windows XP requires only 640 MB of free hard drive space for installation; however, acceptable performance cannot be achieved without 1.5 GB of free space on the Windows XP partition.
- The Readiness Analyzer utility checks hardware and software compatibility. You can also check the Microsoft Web site and manufacturers' Web sites.
- Windows XP supports the same file systems as Windows 2000: FAT16, FAT32, and NTFS.
- You can install Windows XP as a dual boot with Windows 2000, because they both use the same version of NTFS. To dual boot Windows XP with Windows 9x or Windows NT, you must use FAT32. Always install the other OS first, and install Windows XP on a different partition than another OS.
- A clean install is required if you plan to dual boot Windows XP with another OS. Perform an upgrade if you have another version of Windows installed and you do not plan to dual boot.
- Before upgrading to Windows XP, clean up the hard drive by deleting unnecessary files and running Disk Defragmenter and ScanDisk, uncompress the drive, and delete known incompatible software.
- An Express Upgrade uses existing folders and settings as much as possible. A Custom Upgrade allows you to changes folders, language, and the file system.
- Unlike earlier versions of Windows, Windows XP is aware of applications installed under another OS when it is installed as a dual boot.
- Microsoft uses product activation to prevent the use of its software products, including Windows XP, on more than one computer.
- The User State Migration Tool (USMT) enables a user to make a smooth transition from one computer to another by transferring user files and settings. The Scanstate and Loadstate commands accomplish the same thing from the command prompt.
- The Automated System Recovery (ASR) process creates a backup and an ASR floppy disk that can be used to restore the backup of the volume or logical drive holding Windows XP.
- Differences in the Windows XP desktop from earlier versions include the absence (by default) of any shortcuts other than the Recycle Bin and more graphical organization of the Start menu.

- In the Windows XP Control Panel, you can view applications in Category View or Classic View, which is the way it looked in earlier versions of Windows.
- Windows XP allows more than one user to be logged on at the same time, each with his own instances of open applications.
- Windows XP offers processes to help in finding updates for a driver, rolling back a driver if an update fails, and verifying that a driver is certified by Microsoft.
- The Computer Management, Disk Management, and Device Manager tools work much the same way in Windows XP as they did in Windows 2000.
- Windows XP Device Manager hides legacy devices (non-Plug and Play devices) by default.
- You can only install software in Windows XP if you have administrator privileges.
- DOS applications and older Windows applications that did not work under earlier versions of Windows are more likely to work under Windows XP.
- Compatibility mode in Windows XP provides an application written for Windows 9x or later with the environment for which it was designed.
- Two recovery tools new to Windows XP are Automated System Recovery and System Restore.
- The Windows XP System Restore utility is similar to ScanReg in earlier versions of Windows but cannot be executed at a command prompt. System Restore restores the system state using restore points, which are snapshots of the system state.
- Dr. Watson stores information about application errors in the log file Drwatson.log.
- Whereas Windows 2000 included two versions of the Registry Editor, Windows XP includes only one (Regedit.exe) but lets you access it under either name that you used in Windows 2000.

KEY TERMS

Automated System Recovery (ASR) — The Windows XP process that allows you to restore an entire hard drive volume or logical drive to its state at the time the backup of the volume was made.

Compatibility Mode — A Windows XP utility that provides an application with the older Microsoft OS environment it was designed to operate for.

Drwatson.log — The log file for the Dr. Watson utility in Windows XP.

product activation — The process that Microsoft uses to prevent software piracy. For example, once Windows XP is activated for a particular computer, it cannot be installed on another computer.

Remote Assistance — A Windows XP feature that allows a support technician at a remote location to have full access to the Windows XP desktop.

restore point — A snapshot of the system state, usually made before installation of new hardware or applications.

Sigverif.exe — A Windows XP utility that scans device drivers to see whether they are digitally signed. To run the utility, enter the command in the Run dialog box.

System Restore — A Windows XP utility, similar to the ScanReg tool in earlier versions of Windows, that is used to restore the system to a restore point. Unlike ScanReg, System Restore cannot be executed from a command prompt.

User State Migration Tool (USMT) — A Windows XP utility that helps you migrate user files and preferences from one computer to another in order to help a user transition smoothly from one computer to another.

REVIEW QUESTIONS

1. Name the three main versions of Windows XP.
2. What are at least three similarities between Windows XP and Windows 2000? At least three differences?
3. Which operating system is more likely to crash: Windows 9x or Windows XP?
4. What is the difference between joining a workgroup and joining a domain?
5. How much free space on a partition does Windows XP require for installation? How much does it require for acceptable operation?
6. What is the difference between the tools ASR and System Restore?
7. List two different ways to check hardware and software compatibility for Windows XP.
8. What file system do you use if you are installing Windows XP as a dual boot with Windows 9x? Windows NT? Windows 2000?
9. Name at least four things you should do before performing an upgrade to Windows XP.
10. What are the two upgrade options for Windows XP? Explain the difference between them.
11. How long do you have to activate Windows XP? What happens if you don't?
12. What is the first Microsoft product to use product activation?
13. Explain the purpose of the USMT utility and list the three steps needed to use it.
14. What two commands can you use from the command prompt to perform the same functions as the Files and Settings Transfer Wizard?
15. How are Dr. Watson and the Registry Editor different in Windows XP from how they were in Windows 2000?
16. How are the Windows XP desktop and Start menu different from those in Windows 2000?
17. Give two different ways to create shortcuts in Windows XP.
18. What are two ways you can access the Windows XP Device Manager?
19. Name the two files that are needed to copy an older driver from another PC or a backup medium to your Windows XP PC for a device driver rollback.
20. What is the path for the report file created when you run Readiness Analyzer?
21. Which OS are DOS applications more likely to work under: Windows 2000 or Windows XP?
22. List at least three things you can do if a legacy application does not start up and run correctly after you install it under Windows XP.

23. Place these tools in the order in which you should try them when troubleshooting the boot process: Recovery Console, Advanced Options Menu, System Restore.
24. What is a restore point, and what is it used for?
25. Scanreg has been replaced by System Restore in Windows XP. What is the main advantage that Scanreg has over System Restore?
26. Can you use an MS-DOS startup disk to launch Windows XP? To recover data files? To recover from a failed installation of Windows XP?
27. When trying to restore a failed system, what should you do next if Recovery Console does not work?
28. What legacy applications should you not attempt to run under Windows XP?
29. Where should you place a shortcut if you want the associated application to start automatically on startup for all users? Give the entire path.
30. What are two recovery tools new to Windows XP that are used to recover from a failed boot?

HANDS-ON PROJECTS

Problem Solving Using the Microsoft Knowledge Base

Your hard drive has been attacked by a malicious virus and you have decided to restore it from the last backup made by the ASR backup process, but you cannot find the ASR floppy disk required for the restore process. Search the Microsoft Knowledge Base for the steps to recreate the ASR floppy disk when the ASR backup is available. Print the Knowledge Base article.

Using Shortcuts

Create a shortcut on your desktop to Notepad (Notepad.exe), a text editor. Using a second method for creating shortcuts, add a shortcut to the Windows command prompt (Cmd.exe). First, locate the two program files on your hard drive by clicking Start, Search and using the Search dialog box. Then create the shortcuts. List the steps you took to create each shortcut.

Using System Restore

Create a restore point. Make a change to the display settings. Restore the system using System Restore. Are the changes still in effect? Why, or why not?

Using the ASR Process

Create an ASR backup following directions in this guide. Add a few data files to the hard drive. Restore the system using the ASR process. Do the data files still exist on the hard drive? Why, or why not?

Prepare for an Upgrade

On a PC with Windows 2000 or an earlier version of Windows installed, run the Readiness Analyzer from the Windows XP CD to determine whether the PC is ready for Windows XP installation. Make a list of any hardware or software components that are found to be incompatible with Windows XP, and draw up a plan for getting the system ready for an XP upgrade.

Case Project

Install Windows XP

CAUTION

This project will erase everything on your hard drive. Do not do it if you have important data on the hard drive.

Prepare your hard drive for a clean installation of Windows XP by formatting the hard drive. Follow the instructions in the chapter to install Windows XP. Put Windows XP in a partition that is 2 GB in size. Write down each decision you had to make as you performed the installation. If you get any error messages during the installation, write them down and also list the steps you took to recover from the error. How long did the installation take?

Once you have installed Windows XP, use Disk Management to partition and format the remainder of the hard drive. Print a screen shot of Disk Management showing the two partitions. Create an ASR backup of the system partition in the second partition. Print a screen shot showing the files on the ASR floppy disk, using Windows Explorer to view the files.

CHAPTER TWENTY-ONE

21

UNDERSTANDING AND SUPPORTING WINDOWS XP

Labs included in this chapter

Lab 21.1 Allow Two Users to Log on Simultaneously

Objectives

The goal of this lab is to help you understand Windows XP's support for multiple logons. After completing this lab, you will be able to:

- Create a user account which should have administrative privileges
- Log on as two different users simultaneously
- Customize desktop settings for both users
- Switch between two user accounts that are both logged on to the system

Materials Required

This lab will require the following:

- Windows XP operating system

Activity Background

Windows XP includes a new feature that allows more than one user to be logged on to the same computer at the same time, each with his or her own preferences set and programs open. This is useful when more than one person needs to use the same computer. In this lab, you will create a new user account, log onto that account, open a program, change desktop settings, switch back to your own account, and observe the effects of switching between the two user accounts.

Estimated completion time: **30 minutes**

Activity

Follow these steps to create a new user account and open an application using the new account:

1. Log on to your computer under your user account.
2. In the Start menu, right-click **My Computer** and choose **Manage** from the shortcut menu.
3. The Computer Management console opens. Click the **plus sign (+)** next to **Local Users and Groups** to expand it.
4. Under Local Users and Groups, right-click the **Users** folder and choose **New User** from the shortcut menu. The New User dialog box opens.
5. In the New User dialog box, enter a user name, full name, description, and password for your new user. Deselect the **User must change password at next logon** check box, and then select the **User cannot change password**

and **Password never expires** check boxes. (The remaining check box disables the account, which you do not need to do at this time.) Record the user name, full name, and password here:

____

____

6. Click the **Create** button to create the new user account, and then click **Close** to close the New User Dialog box.
7. Double-click the **Users** folder so that the list of users on your computer appears in the right-hand pane of the Computer Management console, and verify that the new user is listed.
8. Open Microsoft Word, WordPad, or some other application.

Follow these steps to switch between users and make changes as the new user:

1. In the Start menu, click the **Log Off** icon and then answer these questions:
   - What options does the Log Off Windows dialog box provide?

     ____

   - Hold your mouse pointer over the **Switch User** icon. If balloon text is enabled on your system, some balloon text appears. If the balloon text appears, write down the keyboard shortcut for switching users.

     ____

2. Click the **Switch User** icon. The login screen appears, just as it does when you first turn the computer on and log on to your account. The new user you just created should be listed. Click the icon for that user's name and enter the password for the user when prompted.
3. Now that you are logged on as the new user, open the **Display Properties** window and change the desktop background for this user. Next, open an application other than the one you opened earlier. For instance, you might open Microsoft Excel or Notepad.
4. Choose **Log Off** from the Start menu again and click **Switch User** to display the logon screen.
   - What information is listed under your user name and under the new user's name?

     ____

     ____

5. Switch back to your user name, and then switch back to the new user again.
   - Does the desktop background change for each user? Do the users' programs remain open?

   ____

6. While logged on as the new user, choose **Turn Off Computer** from the Start Menu and then click the **Turn Off** button.
   - What message do you receive?

   ____

   ____

7. Choose **No** on the dialog box that appeared when you tried to turn off the computer. You return to the new user's desktop.
8. Now you are ready to log off. To do that, click **Log Off** in the Start menu again. Then, in the Log Off Windows dialog box, click **Log Off** instead of **Switch User**. The logon window reappears.
   - What information appears under your user name now? What information appears under the new user's name?

   ____

   ____

Review Questions

1. How do you think the process of switching between users would have been different if you did not assign the user a password? How would it have been different if you had required the user to change the password at the next logon?

   ____

   ____

2. When multiple users are logged on to the same computer, does the logon screen show which programs each user has open? Why do you think this is so?

   ____

   ____

3. What are three advantages to multiple logons?

____

____

____

4. List the steps required to render the new user's account inactive without deleting it. After the account has been rendered inactive, would the user still be listed on the logon screen? Explain.

____

____

____

____

5. In what situation might it be appropriate to disable a user account?

____

____

Lab 21.2 Restore the State System

Objectives

The goal of this lab is to help you restore the system state on a Windows XP computer. After completing this lab, you will be able to:

- Create a restore point using System Restore
- Change system settings
- Restore the system state using the restore point you created

Materials Required

This lab will require the following:

- Windows XP operating system

Activity Background

The System Restore tool in Windows XP enables you to restore the system to the time a snapshot, called a restore point, was taken of the system state. The settings recorded in a restore point include system settings, configuration, and files necessary for a successful boot. When the system state is restored from a restore point, user data on the hard drive is not affected, but software and hardware might be. Restore points are useful if, for example, something goes wrong with a software or hardware installation. In this lab you will create a restore point, make changes to system settings, and then use the restore point to restore the system state.

Estimated completion time: **30 minutes**

ACTIVITY

To use the System Restore tool to create a restore point, follow these steps:

1. On the Start menu, point to **All Programs**, point to **Accessories**, point to **System Tools**, and then click **System Restore**.
2. The System Restore window appears, giving you two choices: Restore my computer to an earlier time and Create a restore point. The first option restores your computer to an existing restore point. Read the information on the left side of the window and answer these questions:
   - Can changes made by System Restore be undone? What type of data does System Restore leave unaffected?

     ____

   - What is the term for the restore points that the system creates automatically?

     ____

   - As you've read, it's helpful to create a restore point before you install software or hardware. In what other situations might you want to create a restore point?

     ____

     ____

3. Click the **Create a restore point** option button and click the **Next** button.
4. In the next window, type a description of the restore point. The description should be something that makes it easy to identify the restore point at a later time.
5. Click the **Create** button.
6. A message appears indicating that the restore point was created. The date, time, and name of the restore point are also shown. Click the **Close** button.

Next, you'll make two changes to the system: uninstalling a Windows component and changing display settings. First, you will uninstall the MSN (Microsoft Network) Explorer component. (If this is currently not installed, then ask your instructor which Windows component you should uninstall instead.)

1. From the Control Panel, double-click the **Add or Remove Programs** icon.
2. The Add or Remove Programs window appears. To see a list of Windows components, click the **Add/Remove Windows Components** icon.
3. The Add or Remove Programs window remains open, and the Windows Components Wizard launches. In the list box in the middle of the screen, components that are checked are currently installed. Scroll down until you see the **MSN Explorer** component and then click the check box next to its name.
4. A message appears asking whether you want to uninstall this component. Click **Yes** to continue.
5. The message disappears, and the MSN Explorer check box is deselected. Click **Next** to continue.
6. A progress window indicates the component the system is currently uninstalling. When the process is complete, a message appears indicating that you have completed the Windows Components Wizard. Click **Finish**.
7. Click **Close** in the Add or Remove Programs Window.

Next, you will change some display settings:

1. From the Control Panel, double-click the **Display** icon.
2. The Display Properties window appears. Click the **Desktop** tab.
3. In the Background list, click a background and then click the **OK** button.
4. The Display Properties window closes. Close the Control Panel window. Notice that the background has changed to the one you selected.

Follow these steps to use the restore point you created to restore the system state:

1. Open the System Restore tool as specified earlier in this lab.
2. Click the **Restore my computer to an earlier time** option button and click **Next**.
3. A window appears showing a calendar of the current month, with the current date highlighted and all dates on which restore points were made shown in bold. Answer these questions:
   - How many restore points were created in the current month?

     ____

- Click each bold date and list the reasons why the restore points were made.

4. Click the current date. In the list on the right, click the name of the restore point you created earlier in the lab, and then click **Next**.
5. A confirmation screen appears. Click **Next** to continue.
   - Describe what happens when you click the Next button.

6. After the system restarts, click your login name to return to the Windows XP desktop. A message appears indicating that the restoration is complete.
   - Did the display settings change back to their original settings?

   - Access the Windows Components Wizard as you did earlier in this lab. Is MSN Explorer installed?

Review Questions

1. List three situations in which you might want to create a restore point.

2. What types of restore points are created by the system, and what types are created by the user?

____

____

3. How often does the system automatically create restore points?

____

____

4. Can more than one restore point be made on a specific date?

____

5. Which of your changes was reversed when you used the restore point to restore the system state, and which change was not reversed? Explain why you think this happened.

____

____

____

Lab 21.3 Install Recovery Console as an Option on the Startup Menu

Objectives

The goal of this lab is to help you install the Recovery Console as a startup option. After completing this lab, you will be able to:

- Install the Recovery Console
- Open the Recovery Console from the Startup Menu

Materials Required

This lab will require the following:

- Windows XP operating system
- Windows XP installation CD or installation files at another location accessible by a drive letter, as specified by your instructor.

Activity Background

The Recovery Console tool in Windows XP allows you to start the computer when other startup and recovery options, such as System Restore, safe mode, and the ASR (Automated System Recovery) process, do not work. In the Recovery Console, you can format a hard drive, copy files from a floppy disk or CD to the hard drive, start and stop certain system processes, and perform other administrative tasks. If the Recovery Console is not installed on your computer, you'll have to run it from the Windows XP installation CD. This lab shows you how to install the Recovery Console on your Windows XP computer so that it appears as an option when the computer starts up.

Estimated completion time: **30 minutes**

Activity

Follow these steps to install the Recovery Console as a startup option:

1. Insert the Windows XP installation CD into your CD-ROM drive. If the Autorun feature launches, close it. If your instructor has given you an alternate location of the installation files, what is the drive letter required to access them?

   ____

2. Click the **Start** button on the taskbar, and then click **Run**. The Run dialog box opens.
3. Type **cmd** and then click **OK**. A command window opens.
4. To switch to your CD-ROM drive (or other drive holding the installation files), type the drive letter followed by a colon and then press **Enter**.
5. You will now execute the Windows XP setup program stored on this drive. The path to the program might vary depending on the release of Windows XP you are using. Here are three possibilities. Try each one until you locate and execute the program:
   - Type **\i386\winnt32.exe /cmdcons** and then press **Enter**.
   - Type **\english\winxp\pro\i386\winnt32.exe /cmdcons** and press **Enter**.
   - Type **\english\winxp\home\i386\winnt32.exe /cmdcons** and press **Enter**.
   - Which command launched the setup program?

   ____

6. A message appears asking if you want to install the Recovery Console. Click **Yes** to continue.

7. The Windows Setup window opens and shows that Setup is checking for updates. When the update check completes, a progress indicator appears. When the installation is complete, a message appears indicating that the Recovery Console was successfully installed. Click **OK** to continue.
8. Restart your computer.
9. When the startup menu appears, select **Microsoft Recovery Console** and press **Enter**. What do you see when the Recovery Console launches?

____

____

____

____

10. Type **1** (to choose to log on to your Windows installation) and then press **Enter**.
11. When prompted, type the administrator password for your computer and press **Enter**.
12. Type **help** and then press **Enter** to see a list of commands available in the Recovery Console.
13. Type **Exit** to close the Recovery Console and restart the computer.

Review Questions

1. What is the advantage of being able to access the Recovery Console from your hard drive instead of from the CD drive?

____

____

2. What is another way to exit the Recovery Console without logging on to your Windows installation?

____

3. In the Recovery Console, what command deletes a directory? What command can you use to list services that are running?

____

4. Name at least two tasks that you might not be able to complete from within the Recovery Console.

____

____

____

5. Why is an administrator password needed for access to the Recovery Console?

____

6. Why should you use the Recovery Console only after other tools have failed?

____

____

Lab 21.4 Use Recovery Console to Copy Files

Objectives

The goal of this lab is to help you learn how to copy files using the Recovery Console. After completing this lab, you will be able to:

- Copy files from a floppy disk to your hard drive using the Recovery Console.

Materials Required

This lab will require the following:

- Windows XP operating system
- Floppy disk

Activity Background

The Windows XP Recovery Console is useful when you need to restore system files after they have been corrupted (perhaps by a virus) or accidentally deleted from the hard drive. In this lab, you will use the Recovery Console (which you installed in Lab 21.3) to restore a system file, System.ini, from a floppy disk. (Windows XP does not need this file to boot; it is included in Windows XP to allow for backward compatibility with older Windows software.)

Estimated completion time: **30 minutes**

Activity

Follow these steps to copy the file System.ini to a floppy disk and then copy it from the floppy to the hard drive using the Recovery Console:

1. Insert the floppy disk in the floppy drive.
2. Using Windows Explorer, locate the file **System.ini** (which is usually found in the C:\Windows folder).
3. Copy the file **System.ini** to the floppy disk and then eject the floppy disk from the drive.
4. Locate **System.ini** on your hard drive again and rename it as **System.old**. When prompted, click **Yes** to confirm that you want to rename the file.
5. Restart the computer again, this time choosing the **Recovery Console**.
6. Insert the floppy disk in the floppy disk drive in the Recovery Console, log on using the Administrator password and type this command: **copy a:\system.ini c:\windows\system.ini**. This command will copy System.ini from the floppy disk to its original location (C:\Windows).
7. Press **Enter**. What message does Recovery Console display?

   ____

8. If C:\Windows is not the active directory, change to that directory and then use the **dir** command to view the contents of the directory. Verify that System.ini was copied to this directory. You might have to use the spacebar to scroll down.
9. Exit the Recovery Console and restart the computer again.

Review Questions

1. You could have used the Recovery Console to rename the System.old file instead of copying the original version from the floppy disk. What command would you have used to perform this task?

   ____

   ____

2. Assume you moved the System file to the My Documents folder. What command would you use in the Recovery Console to move it back to the C:\Windows folder?

____

____

3. When might it be useful to be able to copy files from a CD to the hard drive using the Recovery Console?

____

____

4. Why does Windows XP include the System.ini file?

____

____

5. When might you want to use Recovery Console to copy files from the hard drive to a floppy disk?

____

____

Lab 21.5 Monitor the Memory Counter

Objectives

The goal of this lab is to help you monitor the memory counter to determine a possible memory shortage. After completing this lab, you will be able to:

- Add memory counters to System Monitor
- Defragment your hard drive
- Analyze memory usage during defragmentation

Materials Required

This lab will require the following:

- Windows XP operating system

Activity Background

In Windows XP, you can use the System Monitor utility to observe system performance. You can add counters to Windows XP in order to collect data about the system. In this activity, you will add and monitor counters that measure available memory, memory paging, and the read and write times for disk access. These counters can help you determine how much of the total system resources a particular process (such as defragmenting the hard drive) is using.

Estimated completion time: **30 minutes**

Activity

Lab Activity

Follow these steps to add counters to System Monitor:

1. Click **Start** on the task bar, point to **All Programs**, point to **Administrative Tools** and then click **Performance**. (If Administrative Tools does not appear on your All Programs menu, you need to add it. To do this, right-click the Start menu, click Properties, click the Start menu tab on the Properties window, click Customize, click the Advanced tab in the Customize window, scroll down to System Administrative tools, click Display on the All Programs menu, and then click OK in both windows. After adding Administrative Tools to the All Programs menu, begin again with Step 1.)
2. The Performance console opens. Make sure that System Monitor is selected in the left pane. In the right pane, right-click in the blank area, and then click **Add Counters** in the shortcut menu.
3. The Add Counters window opens. In the Performance object drop-down list, click the **Memory** object. Scroll down the **Select counters from list** scroll box, click the **Available Bytes** counter and then click the **Add** button. This adds the selected counter (Available Bytes) to the Performance console.
4. Click the **Explain** button and record the explanation of the selected counter (Available Bytes) here:

   ____

   ____

5. Repeat step 3 to add the **Pages/sec** counter for the Memory object, the **Processor Time** counter for the Processor object, and the **Disk Read Time** and **Disk Write Time** counters for the Physical Disk object. Record the explanations of each of these counters here:

 ____

 ____

 ____

 ____

6. Click the **Close** button in the Add Counters window. You return to the Performance Console, where the counters you added are listed in the right pane. Look in the Color column and make sure each counter is monitored using a different color. (If you find any of the colors difficult to read, you can change them. To change the color of the line indicating a particular counter, left-click the counter once to select it, then right-click it, select **Properties** from the shortcut menu, click a color in the Color drop-down list on the Properties window, and then click **OK**.)

Follow these steps to monitor the counters for two different applications:

1. With the Performance window still open, open the **Notepad** application. Wait a few seconds, and then close it again.
2. In the Performance window, click the **Freeze Display** button (a red circle with a white x) and then click the highlight button (a light bulb). Use the up and down arrows to move between counters in the list below the performance display.
   - How did the display change when you highlighted a particular counter?

     ____

     ____

   - Which resources did Notepad use primarily? What other resources did it use?

     ____

     ____

3. Close the Notepad application.
4. Click **Start** on the task bar, point to **Administrative Tools**, and then click **Computer Management**.

5. The Computer Management console opens. Under "Storage" in the left pane, click **Disk Defragmenter** and then click **Analyze** in the right pane. What message appears when the analysis is complete?

____

____

6. Click **Close** to close the message window.
7. Close the Computer Management console and return to the Performance window. Click the **Freeze Display** button and the highlight button as you did for Notepad. Which resources did Disk Defragmenter use primarily? Which other resources did it use?

____

____

Review Questions

1. Did Notepad and Disk Defragmenter use the same resources? Why do you think this is so?

____

____

2. How do you think the performance display might have changed if both applications had been open at once?

____

____

3. What are some other counters that could be useful for monitoring system performance?

____

____

4. What system resources that you were monitoring might have been used if you had actually proceeded to defragment your hard drive?

____

____

5. If you were considering whether to upgrade your system's memory or processor, which counters would you choose to monitor and why? How would you decide whether you needed to make the upgrade or not?

____

____

____

____